Are Trams Socialist?

PERSPECTIVES

Series editor: Diane Coyle

Are Trams Socialist?

Why Britain Has No Transport Policy

Christian Wolmar

LONDON PUBLISHING PARTNERSHIP

Published by London Publishing Partnership
www.londonpublishingpartnership.co.uk

Published in association with
Enlightenment Economics
www.enlightenmenteconomics.com

ISBN: 978-1-907994-56-2 (pbk)

A catalogue record for this book is
available from the British Library

This book has been composed in Candara

Copy-edited and typeset by
T&T Productions Ltd, London
www.tandtproductions.com

Printed by Page Bros, Norwich

Contents

Gothenburg tram. Photo by Diane Coyle.

Preface

Transport was a bit of an afterthought in the creation of the UK's system of governance. There was no government department responsible for all aspects of transport until the creation of the Ministry of Transport in the aftermath of World War I, and in its various successive incarnations the transport ministry has never been granted the kind of importance that such weighty matters as finance, defence or home affairs have been accorded. Transport remains low on the list of government priorities – a fact made clear by the small number of transport secretaries whose names have earned a place in the history books. Barbara Castle and possibly Alistair Darling are exceptions, but who, for example, knows that dear old Alfred Barnes, MP for the oddly named East Ham South constituency, held the post throughout the whole Attlee administration?

This lack of prominence for the transport ministry is politically significant. Sure, there is the occasional big scheme, such as the arrival of a new fleet of trains or the opening of a stretch of road, where ministers cut ribbons and give speeches emphasizing the importance of transport, but for the most part it is a backyard ministry populated by politicians on the way up or, more usually, on the way out. Yet transport is a key feature of almost everyone's lives almost every day. Step outside your front door and you are faced with decisions determined by the policies of successive transport ministers, overseen, of course, by the Treasury. Transport, in other words, does not get the attention it deserves.

This short book, therefore, is an attempt to examine how this situation came about, and it considers why there has never been anything approaching a coherent transport policy in this country. By looking at the history of transport over the past century or so, I have tried to explain why there has been so little progress in establishing a policy that takes into account the importance for all of us of the accessibility of places of work, leisure or education and that takes into account the damaging effects of transport on the environment, and its potential negative impact on people's lives, through air pollution, for example. Developing such a coherent policy is, of course, not an easy task, but some 200 years after the Industrial Revolution gave us the means, and created the need, for us to travel, we could have made a better fist of it by now. It is never too late to make a start.

Acknowledgements

My thanks to Jon Shaw, Ian Docherty and Peter Kain for reading through earlier drafts and making many useful suggestions.

Chapter 1

Why railways?

Mass transport is a relatively new phenomenon. For most of human existence, people remained near to where they were born for their entire lives. They might roam to hunt or to seek food, but as agriculture developed settled lives became the norm. Why face the dangers of wandering around if you had a stable food supply nearby and the support of your tribe? There were exceptions – such as soldiers and sailors, and the occasional nomadic tribe – but for the most part the sheer difficulty of travel meant that it posed an unnecessary and unwanted risk. Walking routes were crude or non-existent, the sea was dangerous and horses were only for the relatively affluent (and were not, in any case, suitable for all climates).

The Romans were keen on transport and created a system of roads across much of Europe including Britain, mostly for military reasons but also for trade. But after they left, in the fourth century, no one much bothered about the road network and precious little was done to maintain it during the subsequent 1,500 years.

The condition of the roads and the lack of any cheap and efficient means of undertaking journeys on them meant that travel was limited to the desperate and the affluent, and even the latter did not enjoy the experience. When Archduke Charles – who later became the Holy Roman Emperor Charles VI – visited England in December 1703, his journey from London to Petworth House in Sussex, a mere fifty miles, took a gruelling three days. Indeed, he was lucky to survive the experience as his carriage overturned a dozen times as it slithered and skidded in the icy mud. Conditions in towns were even worse. The *Gentleman's Magazine* described in 1756 how the Mile End Road in London's East End 'resembled a stagnant lake of deep mud'. It would have been a smelly one, too, as thousands of animals were driven along the main roads into central London to be slaughtered at Smithfield Market.

The inadequacy of the roads was partly due to the fact that they were the responsibility of local parishes, which had neither the money nor the will to keep them in good repair. In response to the dire state of the main roads, a system of toll roads, called turnpikes, emerged in the eighteenth century. The turnpike trusts were allowed by parliament to charge for the use of their roads and were supposed to ensure they were well kept, although the latter part of the deal was often not adhered to.

Stimulated by the continued inadequacy of the roads – and created to serve the needs of the industrial revolution and carry its products – the country's system of canals had a brief heyday. The canal age effectively began in 1757 with the completion of the twelve-mile-long Sankey Brook Navigation (many 'canals' consisted partly or even completely of rivers made navigable through dredging and the creation of stable banks). The purpose of this first canal was to move St Helens coal to Liverpool but other uses, such as giving Cheshire salt manufacturers access to a far larger market, soon began to emerge. The success of the Sankey Brook Navigation and, in particular, the Duke of Bridgewater's canal linking Manchester and Liverpool led to the first of two 'canal manias', which resulted in the creation of a national network of waterways. By reducing the cost of transport by as much as 75%, the system of canals, navigable rivers and coastal shipping that emerged widened the market for manufactured goods and consequently began the economic take-off that was greatly accelerated by the advent of the railways.

The key financial mechanism that enabled the canals to be financed and built was the joint stock company. The concept had been around for centuries (there are competing claims in several European countries to being the first such venture) but the canal age gave confidence to the small investor, given the comfortable returns on these pioneering projects. Consequently, it was private capital, with permission from parliament through the 'Bill process', that created this network.

Some canals did carry passengers but the barges were slow, since they were towed by horses and legged through tunnels by men. This made them unattractive, even compared with the ghastly roads, for long journeys. It was the development of steam engines in the eighteenth century that would transform transport. Gradually they became both smaller and more powerful, and it was initially thought that they would eventually be put on wheels and run on roads. However, there were enormous technical difficulties and early attempts mostly ended in mishap or disaster, such as being driven into a ditch or having a boiler explode.

Crucially, though, it was the awful state of the roads that was a barrier to the development of these steam cars. The roads had to some extent improved thanks to the turnpikes and the inventions of the likes of Thomas Telford and John Macadam, and by the turn of the nineteenth century a journey between London and Edinburgh could, in fair weather, take two days rather than a fortnight, which had been the norm a century earlier. However, the roads were still not robust enough to bear the load of the steam carriages that were being developed by various pioneers. As well as much better roads, to get a workable and reliable steam vehicle to perform well on the road required major improvements in the technology for steering, wheels, suspension, transmission, boiler and engine. These were not forth-coming until much later in the nineteenth century.

There was also hostility from the turnpike trusts to-wards the idea of self-powered steam vehicles on the roads, and they imposed very high charges on them – sometimes fifteen times the amount charged to a horse-drawn cart – because of quite justified fears that they would damage the road surface. Parliament, too, was suspicious, and in 1865 it passed the Locomotive Act, popularly known as the Red Flag Act, setting a speed limit of four miles per hour in rural areas and two miles per hour in towns, as well as the requirement for a person with a red flag to walk ahead of the vehicle to warn horse riders and pedestrians of the approach of a self-propelled machine.

The solution, therefore, was to build a railway – in other words, to provide a permanent way on which the vehicles could travel. Rails could bear a heavier load than roads, and locomotives required little springing because they travelled on a hard smooth surface. Technologi-cal developments – such as more efficient boilers and, crucially, the clever idea of flanged wheels (rather than flanged rails) – also gave railways a key advantage. More-over, they did not require steering: a function that took some time to master. A single steam locomotive on the tracks could pull several wagons or carriages, making it far more economically efficient, and since iron on iron (or steel on steel) generates far less friction than wheels on dirt or even tar roads, it also meant that vehicles on tracks were far more fuel efficient.

For all these negative and positive reasons, it was therefore a collective, rather than individual, form of transport that broke the mould and enabled faster transport for both people and goods. The railways triumphed for the best part of a century, and supporters of cars and their ilk had to bide their time until motor vehicle technology was developed, as had happened with the railways, in a piecemeal way. They would, however, get their revenge.

The railway century

The railway age began, accompanied by considerable fanfare, with the opening of the Liverpool and Manchester Railway in September 1830. There had been numerous cruder predecessors but, in terms of sophistication and technology, the Liverpool and Manchester was groundbreaking in numerous respects: it was double tracked; it used exclusively locomotive power, rather than horse power; it linked two major towns (which later became cities); and it carried both passengers and freight. Numerous early passengers testified to the excitement of going faster than had previously been possible – the speed of a galloping horse was the fastest that anyone had travelled to this point.

Fears of being unable to breathe at such speeds or of being killed by an exploding boiler (a more realistic concern but still a relatively rare occurrence) soon abated and a remarkable period of railway growth ensued. The railway mania of the 1840s resulted in the creation of a network of more than 5,000 miles just two decades after the opening of the Liverpool and Manchester – around half of today's remaining mileage.

Passengers flocked to use the trains. The Great Exhibition of 1851, for example, was an astonishing success, attracting more than six million visitors (a third of the population of England and Wales at the time) from all around the country to London thanks to the railways. Special trains were run from every major regional centre, giving many people their first ever ride on a train.

The railways had arrived as a mass form of transit. They were to be unchallenged for the remainder of the century, meaning that the private firms that owned and operated them were able to amass sufficient capital to enable them both to improve the existing network – speeding up services, building magnificent stations and providing more facilities – and to extend it to every corner of the country, even sparsely populated areas where lines were never likely to return a profit in order to prevent rivals establishing territory. By the turn of the century, the British network had extended to 18,700 miles and average speeds on main lines were generally around forty-five miles per hour. The roads had a minor role, connecting people with the local station by means of horse-drawn carriages or carts, or simply Shanks's pony.

As a means of inter-urban transport, the railways had a virtual monopoly. There were still some stagecoaches but, as can be seen from Sherlock Holmes's encyclopaedic knowledge of the railway timetable as he rushes off to the scene of the latest crime, the railways were the predominant form of travel. While there was some consolidation, and the emergence of a few major railway companies such as the London and North Western and the Great Western, there were still a couple of hundred railway companies at the outset of World War I.

In the cities and major towns the situation was somewhat different. There was an alternative in the form of trams, initially horse drawn but later electrically powered. They were a marked advance on their predecessors: the horse-drawn omnibuses that had appeared on the streets of several cities around the same time as the opening of the Liverpool and Manchester Railway. Omnibuses were slow, inefficient and expensive because of the cost of horses, which not only required expensive feed but also lived short miserable lives as a result of the harsh nature of the work. Consequently, omnibuses were the preserve of the middle classes since they were too expensive to be a genuinely mass form of transport.

Trams, on the other hand, *were* able to cater for the masses. The advantage of trams was similar to that of the railways: since the roads were so bad, laying tracks enabled far more efficient progress. The first horse-drawn trams (coincidentally the brainchild of a man called George Train) appeared in London along the Bayswater Road between Marble Arch and Notting Hill Gate in 1861, but they were a failure.

By the end of the decade, however, tram systems had been laid in Liverpool, Glasgow and Edinburgh, and London saw its first regular tram service running in south London between Brixton and Kennington in 1870. The electrification of trams, which began as early as the 1880s, enabled them to reach their full potential. Even in those early days, electricity proved to be far cheaper than horse traction, and as a result fares were reduced at the same time as services improved. Trams therefore enjoyed a boom and were widely used by the working class, who had hitherto largely been unable to travel distances of any great length to employment except in areas where there happened to be suburban railways, many of which provided cheap 'workmen's trains'.

Cheap tickets had first been offered, to dockers, by Eastern Counties Railway as early as 1847, and by the 1860s numerous railway companies were providing some kind of discounted offer for workers, normally us-able only on early morning[*] and late evening trains. As

---

[*] Cruelly, many of these early morning trains delivered the workers too early for their employers, leaving them to hang around for a couple of hours in the wet and cold.

a consequence, whole London suburbs of cheap hous-ing were built on the basis of the availability of this dis-counted access to employment. These workmen's trains were a great improvement on the previous provision for cheap travel: the requirement under the 1844 Railways Regulation Act for every company to run at least one train per day on every line, serving all stations and cost-ing just one pence per mile.

Tram systems, however, were far cheaper to build and therefore became widespread in many towns that were too small to develop suburban rail services. They offered cheap fares all day long, unlike the railways. They were an early version of a partnership between local au-thorities and private enterprise since they were depend-ent on installing rails in municipally owned streets, for which the private promoters needed to obtain permis-sion. In fact, local authorities soon became the domi-nant partner, helped by the 1870 Tramway Act, which provided for the acquisition of tramway networks by local authorities after a suitable length of ownership by the original private promoter. Over time most tram-way systems – which, incidentally, were highly profita-ble for a time – therefore became municipally owned. This pattern of municipal ownership was initially greatly beneficial for the growth of trams, but eventually, after World War II, it hastened their demise. Trams were not universally welcomed, precisely because they catered for the working classes. The City of London, which had prevented the construction of any mainline stations on its patch, refused to allow trams on its streets, arguing that they 'catered for an undesirable class of person'.[1] It was an attitude that was not confined to the City.

London had the extra benefit of underground railways. The stimulus for the creation of the Underground was the congested nature of London's thoroughfares, epitomized by Doré's famous print of Ludgate Hill with the streets clogged with carriages, costermongers and a throng of people. This was not a new phenomenon. London's streets were narrow, crowded and insanitary, with overhanging buildings and crowded dwellings. They had been this way for centuries and the rebuilding of the city after the Great Fire had been a fantastic missed opportunity. The centres of provincial cities also suffered from overcrowding, though not on the same scale as London.

The Metropolitan Railway between Farringdon and Paddington, completed in 1863, was the world's first underground railway and was built by the simple cut and cover method – essentially digging a hole, putting a railway in it and covering it over. Over the next quarter of a century an extensive network of lines – powered, remarkably, by steam engines, and encompassing today's Circle, District and Metropolitan lines – was built up. The Metropolitan recognized early on the value of providing for the working classes and offered cheap tickets on early morning trains at a third of the normal nine pence return fare.

With too many buildings on London's streets and too many utilities underneath them, a series of deep-level 'Tubes' were cut out of the capital's clay and, by necessity, were also electrically powered since steam would have created a deadly atmosphere in the closed tunnels deep below the city's streets. In the UK, only Glasgow emulated London by creating an underground system, but several cities built up extensive suburban rail networks, some of which survive today. Commuting became a way of life for large swathes of the population.

With technological improvements such as electrification – which was eventually adopted throughout the Underground and began to be introduced on the rail network late in the nineteenth century – and substantial investment thanks to the profits generated by what was often a monopoly situation, the railways enjoyed something of a golden age in the run-up to World War I. Motor buses, replacing their horse-drawn predecessors, were also a great improvement, and tram networks were intensifying. Public transport, operated by a mix of public and private interests, was dominant. And then that most disruptive of technologies, the motor car, arrived, destroying these cosy monopolies and breaking up the established pattern of transport in an unplanned and unpredictable way. The policy response was then, as it is now, inchoate and confused.

Chapter 2

Getting nowhere faster

Today's Lycra-clad cyclists will find it ironic that the roads were initially improved for their more modestly dressed predecessors, who campaigned for the creation of a network that would enable them to enjoy a day's outing without numerous punctures. For a couple of decades from the mid 1870s, cyclists were the fastest travellers on the roads and the two main cycling organizations linked together to form the Roads Improvement Association (RIA), which lobbied for the creation of a network of smooth roads. Cyclists even raised money to pay for road improvements and took recalcitrant highway authorities to court under the Highways Act 1835 for their failure to maintain the roads in a proper state of repair. The lobbying by cyclists was all too successful. County surveyors, terrified by seeing their counterparts humiliated in court, rushed to spend money on making good their highways. A similar process took place in the US, where cyclists also paid for a network of cycle paths and lobbied for road improvements.

For the cyclists, it proved to be a case of turkeys voting for Christmas. The smooth roads were even better suited to cars than bicycles. Consequently, the motoring organizations that the cyclists helped set up were soon lobbying against them and arguing to exclude them from the roads entirely. Worse, some of the keenest cycling lobbyists were also early motorists and soon spurned their former colleagues, lured by the attraction of effortless travel at unprecedented speeds. The roads, which had initially been created largely for pedestrians, were soon excluding them: their main, and sometimes only, purpose was to cater for motor vehicles travelling as fast as possible from A to B. Once the Red Flag Act was repealed in 1896, the triumph of the car was inevitable.

At the outbreak of World War I, there were just over 100,000 private cars registered in the UK, but already the rules of the road were being rewritten in their favour. As Carlton Reid, the chronicler of the history of cycling and roads, put it:

> In just a short space of time cyclists – and pedestrians – became alien and undesirable users of British roads. Alien and undesirable to motorists, that is.[2]

The early motorists speeding through the countryside were not universally welcome. There was no shortage of cartoons in the press depicting these Mr Toads imperilling the lives of country folk and being upbraided. Consequently, the early roads lobby did not have it all their own way. There were plenty of people who objected to the dirt, the dust and the danger, like Evelyn Everett-Green, a prominent turn-of-the-century author, who lived on the main road between Guildford and Dorking and complained to a parliamentary enquiry that drivers 'would go at any speed', with the dust stirred up by their vehicles meaning that 'all her flowers were spoiled and [her] health injured'. She had been forced to move her study to the back of the house because of 'the vibration, the noise and the smell'.[3]

However, the march of the car was unstoppable, not least because it was the rich and the powerful who were able to afford motor vehicles, while the 'lower orders' could often not even afford a bicycle and were restricted to walking and public transport. Motorists were helped by both legislative measures and government policies. The first major legislation, the 1903 Motor Car Act, required cars to be licensed and display a registration number, and it imposed a twenty miles per hour speed limit that was to be implemented by county councils. The crucial element, however, was the gradual acceptance and codification of the notion of 'obstructing the highway': people and animals had to get out of the way of the cars. This prioritization, which survives to this day, underpins the flow of traffic and established today's pattern of urban transport.

The first taxes on motor vehicles were introduced by Chancellor of the Exchequer David Lloyd George in the 1909 budget and consisted of a petrol tax of three pence per gallon and an annual vehicle tax of between £2 2s and £42 depending on the vehicle type and its horsepower. Lloyd George made a key concession to motorists by promising that all the money raised would be spent on improvements to the road network. However, by the mid 1920s his successor, Winston Churchill, was already raiding the fund for general taxation, and eventually, in 1937, the link was formally abandoned, though many advocates for motoring suggest that this hypothecation still exists. Oddly, in his first post-election budget in 2015, the chancellor, George Osborne, suggested that a reformed Vehicle Excise Duty would be earmarked solely for spending on roads.

The naive cycling lobby had pushed for the creation of wide main roads in the expectation that cyclists would then be safer on the minor ones, but, instead, the construction of bypasses and dual carriageways (a quaintly inappropriate word, which is a reminder that cars were initially considered to be carriages) merely encouraged cars to go faster and did little to improve conditions elsewhere. The Roads Improvement Association, which remained influential throughout the interwar period, was responsible for a fundamental change in philosophy. According to Mick Hamer's classic book on the roads lobby, *Wheels within Wheels*, the RIA

> established the philosophy that the roads should be made to suit the traffic. Before the RIA, no single philosophy prevailed.[4]

Indeed, Hamer cites the requirement, before the advent of cars, that wagons had to have large wheels in order to avoid cutting up tracks, and, as he points out,

> the RIA's philosophy, 'that roads should be made to suit the traffic', ruled for the next sixty years.[4]

Measures controlling car use were slower to be introduced. The driving test was not introduced until 1935, and even then it was suspended during World War II and not reintroduced until 1946. The notional speed limit of twenty miles per hour that had been introduced in 1903 was universally disregarded, as noted by a parliamentary inquiry in 1930, which estimated that not one driver in a thousand observed the limit and that, indeed, bus services were timetabled on the basis of travelling faster than the law stipulated. Consequently, the limit was abolished that year but the death toll, already over 6,000 annually, rose alarmingly to 7,343 in 1934, forcing the authorities to create a thirty miles per hour limit in built-up areas. The first drink-driving legislation was introduced in 1925, but a legal threshold of alcohol content in the blood was only introduced in 1967, amid much controversy about country pubs being forced out of business as a result. Wearing a seat belt in the front seats of a car was not made mandatory until 1983, although anchorage points had been a requirement in new cars since the 1960s, and the requirement for rear seat belts was brought in as recently as 1991. Pedestrian crossings were only first established in the mid 1930s.

Much of this was the result of attacks on positive legislation and rearguard action by the roads lobby, which outgrew its origins as the plaything of car-enthusiast aristocrats, such as Lord Montague of Beaulieu, after World War I and became a highly professionalized and influential group that included car manufacturers (protected at the time by an import duty of a third on all vehicles), oil companies, the country's two motoring clubs (the Automobile Association and the Royal Automobile Club), road hauliers, car salesmen and bus companies (notably the biggest: the London General Omnibus Company). At the end of World War I, David Lloyd George, by then prime minister, had wanted to nationalize the railways (supported by Winston Churchill) and incorporate them into the Ministry of Transport, which was already responsible for roads. The motoring lobby baulked at the prospect, concerned that the railway interest would dominate, especially as the inaugural transport minister, Sir Eric Geddes, had been a leading executive of the North Eastern Railway. Therefore, the Automobile

Association and the Society of Motor Manufacturers and Traders lobbied successfully not only to ensure that the legislation specified there should be a separate department within the ministry to deal with roads but also that there would be a committee, made up of representatives of highway authorities and other motoring interests, to advise the minister on matters concerning roads, bridges and other facilities for vehicles. In other words, the power of the roads lobby was actually legally enshrined in the legislation whereas the poor railways were always outsiders looking in.

The ministry of transport in its various successive incarnations has always been riven between the two modes: roads and rail. Ministers have always been characterized as 'roads men' or 'railway men' (there have only ever been three women transport cabinet members and, of them, only Barbara Castle had any lasting impact) and the two sections of the department have traditionally acted separately, even when, as recently, they were supposed to be integrated.

Pushed by the powerful roads lobby and backed by many politicians who embraced the same type of philosophy later expressed so neatly by Nicholas Ridley (one of the most influential of Margaret Thatcher's transport secretaries), between the wars Britain embraced the car wholeheartedly and began to adapt its infrastructure to accommodate this new deity, both within urban areas and between them. The roads lobby won an important battle over the composition of the Ministry of Transport created in the aftermath of the war by ensuring that roads and rail remained separate sections in the ministry. This was to have a lasting impact and remains crucially important even today. As Philip Bagwell and Peter Lyth's *Transport in Britain* explains:

> In the years that followed, road building and motor transport assumed an ever growing importance by comparison with the railways.[5]

This was reflected in the numbers of staff in the ministry who worked on the roads side: by the mid twentieth century they outnumbered their railway colleagues by a factor of at least four to one – a neat illustration of the politicians' priorities.

The demand for road space was soaring. The development of road freight traffic had been stimulated by the cheap availability of ex-army lorries in the aftermath of the war. These were bought cheaply by ex-servicemen, who promptly set up local haulage businesses, taking freight off the railways, which never recovered to their pre-war levels of goods carriage. The General Strike of 1926, when the rail network effectively ground to a halt, also proved a boon to the haulage industry as, mostly not unionized, it kept running for the duration of the action. The number of buses also increased rapidly in the 1920s, mostly run by small outfits, although the railway companies, now consolidated into just four groupings, were eager to stifle competition by using their industrial muscle to enter the bus market.

The newly created Ministry of Transport recognized the need for a network of major roads across the country and started providing funds, partly to relieve unemployment and give the demobbed soldiers work. Progress was, in truth, slow. Before 1937, responsibility for roads, even major arteries, remained with the often-cash-strapped county councils, and road schemes tended to focus on areas of high unemployment rather than on those with the greatest traffic congestion. As such, there was no coherent national plan until the establishment of the trunk road network in 1937: a network that encompassed more than 4,000 miles of road and became the direct responsibility of the ministry. Despite the efforts of the ministry and the roads lobby, the lack of a centralized strategy and the shortage of money in the aftermath of the Depression, the development of Britain's road network lagged behind progress in America and in several European nations, notably Germany, where early types of motorway had started being built.

A rather louche gossip magazine, with the suggestive title of *Tit-Bits*, was to play an unlikely key role in the development of the British motorway network. The County Surveyors Society had begun work on a plan for a 1,000-mile network of motorways and had even sought the advice of their German counterparts. Just before the outbreak of war, the plan – consisting of rather crudely

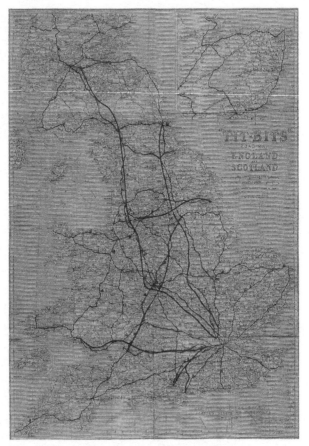

The map that set out Britain's motorway
network (from *Tit-Bits* magazine).

drawn crayon lines on a road map originally published in
Tit-Bits – was presented to the government and became
the basis of the campaign for road improvements.

The war put this lobbying on hold, though there was some activity behind the scenes to ensure that road investment would be given a high priority after the conflict. The British Roads Federation (BRF), which encompassed a wide range of members from across the industry, had now taken on the mantle of leading the roads lobby and pushed vociferously for the *Tit-Bits* scheme. Although there was no money to build roads in the immediate aftermath of the war, the BRF managed to persuade the Labour transport minister, Alfred Barnes, to announce, in May 1946, a ten-year plan to build an 800-mile network of motorways not much different from the scheme set out in *Tit-Bits*. The BRF increased the pressure by distributing 35,000 copies of a pamphlet called 'The case for motorways', which helped ensure the passage of legislation through parliament allowing for the construction of motorways.

Despite the lack of government money (post-war austerity was on a different scale to even the worst aspects of the current version), the BRF continued pressing its case – and it was pushing at an open door. The Conservative government that was elected in 1951 was even more eager than its predecessor to see a major expansion in the roads network, once money allowed. It took up and expanded Labour's motorway programme, with construction soon starting.

In one of those bizarre anomalies beloved of pub quiz question setters, Britain's first motorway, opened in 1958, was the Preston bypass. It was no coincidence that it was located in Lancashire, as the county surveyor, James Drake, had long been an advocate of motorways and had drawn up plans for what essentially became a part of the M6. Plans for several other motorways were taking shape by then, and the arrival at the Ministry of Transport of Ernest Marples, who owned a majority shareholding in the eponymous civil engineering firm, ensured a speeding up of the motorway programme. The pendulum swung even further towards roads and against the railways in 1961 when Marples appointed the notorious axeman, Richard Beeching, to head British Railways, which had been nationalized thirteen years previously.

The shift towards motorization was now in full swing. Once the country started recovering from the austerity of the immediate post-war period, with full employment, rising wages and the relative costs of motoring falling, owning a car became feasible for the middle classes and even for blue-collar workers who were enjoying a period of stable employment. There was, at least initially, a built-in time advantage for drivers. They could get door to door more quickly, given that public transport had to be accessed by walking to a bus stop or station. However, that advantage started being eroded as more and more people took to their cars, causing increasing congestion, a contradiction that was never recognized by policymakers intent on furthering the spread of car ownership, which was seen as desirable in and of itself.

Public transport was reckoned to be of little relevance and suburban rail networks in the provinces were consequently pared back and bus networks were thinned out. All of Britain's tram networks, with the exception of Blackpool's famous seafront route, were closed between the 1930s and the early 1960s. They were seen as getting in the way of cars and as being irrelevant to the needs of the second half of the twentieth century. Manchester's last tram ran in 1949, Liverpool's system was scrapped the following year and London went in 1952, while Birmingham stumbled on till the year after that. Dozens of systems in smaller towns, nearly all of which had become municipally owned as they were loss-making, had gone already. Before the war there had been a few attempts to modernize systems. Leeds, for example, drew up a scheme to put trams in tunnels and allocate more road space for them, but, like all other attempts to improve tram networks, the plan was soon ditched as too expensive. While it was principally the competition for road space from the car that killed off the trams, often it was the need for renovation and the purchase of new trams that made systems unviable in the eyes of the municipal authorities. Many towns and cities in Europe, however – particularly in Eastern Europe, where car ownership was low under Communism, and in northern countries, which had a more enlightened attitude towards public transport – saw the value in keeping alive a system that, by its very nature, had priority over cars.

Trolleybuses, a particularly useful form of public transport as they were quiet and did not emit fumes, as well as being cheaper than trams, were also culled. There were roughly fifty systems around the UK at the peak, and because they required less investment, and were not perceived to be getting in the way of cars quite so much, they survived longer. Many were not closed down until the 1960s, and the schemes in Walsall and Cardiff survived until the start of the 1970s. Again, numerous European cities saw the value in these quiet (if slightly cumbersome) buses and they survive to this day.

Remarkably, the Underground, now such an over-used resource, was also seen as expendable in the post-war period. In researching *The Subterranean Railway,* my history of the London Tube, I discovered that there were several years in the 1950s when the Underground received as little as £300,000 to fund its entire investment programme. Expansions planned before the war were shelved and the much-needed Victoria Line, first mooted in the 1940s, did not see the light of day until 1968. Indeed, after the splurge of lines built in the first decade of the twentieth century, the only other new Tube line opened in the twentieth century was the Jubilee line, built – with a characteristic lack of planning – in two sections twenty years apart. Moreover, in a monument to the incompetence of British transport planning, a section of the line, to Charing Cross, had to be abandoned because the extension was constructed on an alignment not originally envisaged: a fantastic waste of resources given the paucity of investment in the system during this period. It lies gathering dust under a city crying out for more Underground capacity.

Chapter 3

Roads and more roads

The long-term emphasis on roads in transport policy should be viewed in the context of an exceptionalism about British attitudes. Britain has long had a somewhat different attitude towards roads and traffic than its European counterparts, even looking far back in history, and this helps to explain the rapidity with which the new form of traction was allowed to dominate after World War I, especially in urban areas. The town planning academic Carmen Hass-Klau suggests there are key cultural differences between German (and other continental European) and British (and, consequently, Anglo-American, also including Australian, Canadian and New Zealand) attitudes towards road use. She postulates that it is to do with national concepts of freedom and suspicion of state intervention, and this may explain why, for example, British towns and cities have been slow to embrace the kind of pedestrianization schemes that are commonplace on the continent or to try to create the central pedestrianized squares that are so important in giving cities vibrancy. German cities were traditionally more likely to impose controls over the use of wheeled vehicles, especially in narrow streets, out of a Teutonic desire for order. British city rulers tended not to interfere in that way, and in Britain

> there appears to have been (and still is) a greater acceptance of wheeled, and later motor, traffic as a way of life from very early on and a possible fear of conflicts of 'equal rights' of all participants were not provided.[6]

This attitude was later encapsulated by Nicholas Ridley in clear ideological terms:

> The private motorist ... wants the chance to live a life that gives him [sic] a new dimension of freedom – freedom to go where he wants, when he wants, and for as long as he wants.[7]

There is only one thing wrong with this argument, but it is a rather fundamental point: one person's freedom may require another's imprisonment. It is the tragedy of the commons. Road space is a scarce resource and yet there is no price control on it. As has been argued before, in a world of infinite resources and land, the car would be perfect. Traffic jams in space are rare. However, on this planet, and particularly in urban areas, the space available for cars is not limitless. Indeed, it is highly constrained. The road lobby has, therefore, devoted the thrust of its efforts to trying to make it less constrained.

The apogee of this line of thinking was the publication of the Buchanan Report – *Traffic in Towns* – in 1963. The motorways were beginning to tackle the inter-urban traffic jams that regularly hit the headlines, most notoriously on the Exeter bypass in the summer, but the roads in towns were becoming clogged and the congestion was unbearable. Even in relatively small towns, congestion, noise, accidents and fumes were making life in central areas intolerable and were driving people out to the suburbs, where the quality of life was seen as better. It was an irony, then, that enhanced mobility was the start of the decline of many inner city areas – a phenomenon that was of course much more intense and widespread in the US. Better access into city centres also made it easier to get out of them.

Buchanan's report, which was commissioned by the government, was an attempt to adapt towns and cities to the 'full motorization' that he deemed inevitable given the popularity of cars. Interest in the issue was so great that the report was published, in a shortened edition, as a 'Penguin special' that sold tens of thousands of copies.

The key recommendation was the segregation of motor traffic and pedestrians, which inevitably required the construction of a vast network of urban motorways, dual carriageways and feeder roads in every town and city. While Colin Buchanan himself expressed some concerns about the implications of motorization, he was of the view that if you can't beat 'em, join 'em. The forces propelling society towards a car-dominated culture were, he thought, irresistible and had to be accommodated. As he explained in the introduction to the report,

> we concluded, since it is obviously the desire of society to use the motor vehicle to the full, that the only practical basis for a study of the present kind was to accept this desire as a starting point and then to explore and demonstrate its consequences.[8]

In the preface, Sir Geoffrey Crowther, a former editor of *The Economist,* wrote: 'One of the peculiarities of the motor car is that virtually everybody wants to have one.'[9] It was that misconception which was to fuel transport policy throughout this period.

A neat illustration of the Buchanan ideal is the small Berkshire town of Newbury, which he used as an example. He argued that it was essential to build a road network in the town to cope with 'peak car', which entailed the reorganization of towns around this priority. In Newbury, with a population of just 30,000, his estimate was that commuting car numbers would increase threefold, from 3,000 to 9,000. He then admitted that the existing town structure simply could not accommodate this growth:

> We did not construct a peak hour flow diagram for the year 2010 on the basis of the *existing* street system because it was quite obvious that the existing system could not possibly carry the enormously increased loads.[10]

In other words, to meet the needs of the motorists, the whole town centre would have to be destroyed and rebuilt because the urban motorways and what were known as distributor roads (new roads aimed at better 'distributing the traffic') would channel traffic into the traditional main street.

Plymouth: a town centre fashioned for the motorist.
Source: photo by Smalljim (see page 115 for full details).

Plymouth, which had the bad luck of being flattened by German bombers targeting its shipyard, had the further misfortune of being rebuilt precisely on this basis and as a result remains a nightmare to this day for road users and public transport passengers alike. As Ernest Marples, the transport minister in the Conservative government of 1959–64, explained to a British Road Federation conference in 1963, this was to be the norm for towns and cities across the

33

UK because they were laid out in the wrong way to accommodate cars:

> We have to face the fact, whether we like it or not, that the way we have built our towns is entirely the wrong way for motor traffic. We want an entirely different type of town.[11]

Newbury fortunately survived that fate at the time but was, ironically, the subject of a fierce row in the 1990s over the improvement of its bypass, which was eventually built. Imagine, by way of contrast, an Italian transport minister suggesting that the historic centres of Italy's towns and cities be pulled down in order to make space for the growing number of Cinquecentos. They would be ridiculed and laughed out of office, and yet city centres across the UK were ripped out and destroyed to make way for the car far more comprehensively than the Luftwaffe (which had, in places such as Coventry, started the process) had ever achieved.

The most remarkable aspect of the Buchanan Report was its blindness towards other forms of transport. There was no consideration of how accommodating this vast influx of cars would affect bus and rail services. As Kerry Hamilton and Stephen Potter wrote in a book that accompanied a Channel 4 series on transport,

> there was no reference anywhere in the report of the implications this would have for forms of transport other than the private car.[12]

To encourage acceptance of Buchanan's plans, the ministry organized a roadshow to present the findings in cities such as Glasgow, Liverpool and Newcastle upon Tyne and then sent a circular out to local councils exhorting them to draw up 'land use transportation plans', which were, essentially, an American idea that required them to forecast how much traffic there would be and then plan the roads necessary to accommodate that traffic. This was the basis of the now much discredited 'predict and provide' technique, which, in fact, has never been applied to other modes of transport – apart from aviation, and even there the obstacles to airport development have proved to be a constraint. More than a hundred local authorities drew up these land use transportation plans over the next decade, determining the nature of their town planning for a generation.

In the event, the Buchanan Report could not be implemented because of its own internal contradictions. While many towns and cities still bear the hallmarks of failed attempts to worship at Buchanan's altar, none could afford the full Monty. That would simply have required far too much spending in relation to the size of the area the roads would have served and raised the ire of too many local citizens. While the constraints of cost, political opposition and practicality prevented local authorities from adopting the Buchanan thinking *in toto*, many town centres – ranging in size from

Burnley to Birmingham, Leicester to Luton – remain blighted to this day by half-implemented 'Buchananization', with ring roads, dual carriageways and even odd short stretches of motorway creating soulless car-oriented environments that encourage motor vehicles to enter city centres or speed through them, cutting cities in half as decisively as the Berlin wall. Poor Leeds even had 'Motorway city of the seventies' stamped on all outgoing letters as testimony to its adoption of the Buchanan ethic. Buchanan's ideas formed the core of advice from central government to local planners for a couple of decades, and some planners and highway engineers are still influenced by it when drawing up transport schemes today. The nirvana of an urban landscape built to accommodate the car remains a dream for the true believers.

It was London, though, that became the subject of the most ambitious motorization plan, but it was a scheme that proved to be Buchanan's nemesis. London, with its enormous traffic jams and its narrow streets, had been subjected to many 'solutions' by planners and politicians. Ensuring cars could get into central London was seen as vital to the national interest and the functioning of the economy. The scheme that best illustrated this was the transformation of Park Lane, the short road that runs for a bit less than a mile between Hyde Park Corner and Marble Arch, into a dual carriageway with four lanes in both directions. This took some effort on the part of politicians, since it required nabbing a twenty-acre section out of Hyde Park, a Royal Park, but was justified by the transport minister, John Boyd Carpenter, because

> no single road development scheme could make a greater contribution to the relief of growing traffic congestion.[13]

Savour that statement for a moment. This was more important than motorways, dual carriageways, bypasses and any country roads. More important than trains, buses and planes. The priority, according to Boyd Carpenter, was to get people into the centre of London as quickly as possible. Nothing encapsulates the thinking of the period better than the establishment in 1961 of Britain's first drive-in bank: a branch of Drummonds (now Royal Bank of Scotland) in Trafalgar Square. The thinking, therefore, was that it was desirable for people to drive into the city centre in order to carry out banking operations without getting out of their cars: a neat illustration of the contradictions and lack of reality of these car-based ideas. Fortunately, the drive-in bank did not catch on and soon disappeared.

In the event, taking out a chunk of the Royal Parks was not enough for the likes of Boyd Carpenter. A much more ambitious scheme to solve London's traffic problems once and for all was in the offing. A plan for a series of ring roads in and around London was first mooted in the 1940s, but it was not until Marples was installed as transport minister in 1959 that the government began to seriously plan them. The favoured idea was for three concentric 'motorway boxes': the outer one became the M25 and the middle one was essentially a revamped north and south circular. It was the inner one – an urban motorway, largely on stilts, running in a 3–4 mile circle from Charing Cross – that was most controversial. At first the scheme was quietly developed away from the public gaze by a team of road engineers working jointly for the ministry and the Greater London Council (GLC) with the support of both main political parties. Once information about the plan began to be made public, however, there was growing opposition. The plan would have involved the demolition of at least 20,000 homes, which was seen as unproblematic by the British Road Federation because, according to evidence the organization gave to the GLC, 'much of the route lies in obsolete areas which urgently need rebuilding'. That was not the way that residents of Battersea, Hampstead, Chelsea and Blackheath viewed their local areas. It was precisely because the road, which would have had eight lanes in some sections, would have destroyed parts of these affluent and middle-class areas of London that the project was probably always doomed.

However, a section of it was built. Motorists wondering why they are 'blessed' with a half-mile section of motorway (barely long enough to reach the seventy mile an hour speed limit) north of Shepherds Bush roundabout in West London can thank the promoters of the motorway boxes, even if all it succeeds in doing is getting them to the inevitable jams on the A40 more quickly. It was the sight of that motorway and the linked two-and-a-half-mile Westway spur into central London that roused considerable protest – not least on the day in 1970 that it was opened by Michael Heseltine – and ensured that the project would eventually be shelved permanently. It was not until 1971, though, when the Labour party changed its mind and came out against the ringways, that the project started to fall apart. The issue featured prominently in the 1973 GLC election, and the victorious Labour party soon scrapped the two innermost ringways, but it had no power to stop the outer one, which was eventually built as the M25, as it was routed outside the capital's boundaries.

It would be naive to say that the popularity of the car and its primary place in planning were purely the result of the policies of a few politicians and civil servants. The car was popular and its negative effects were not always apparent. It was still possible in the 1960s, and possibly even in the 1970s, 'to go for a drive' in the countryside and enjoy the experience. Owning a car seemed to offer unparalleled freedom and unlimited potential to travel. However, it was the alacrity with which the likes of Buchanan supported the notion of the car as the solution to all problems of mobility without any understanding of the context or of the limitations that was so damaging and so at odds with thinking elsewhere in Europe, where there was in many places a far more measured approach. They may still use their cars, but, because there is decent public transport, Europeans can also make use of an alternative. In other words, spending on public transport has increased, not decreased, their options.

Chapter 4

Love and hate on the tracks

The loss of the motorway boxes marked a turning point in transport history. It made clear that there were limits to motorization and that, in urban areas particularly, a policy of trying to enable unlimited access to the car was bound to fail. It was not just in London that the penny had dropped. Across Britain in the late 1970s, public inquiries into road schemes were being disrupted by anti-roads campaigners, who combined direct action with playing the Department of Transport at its own game by mugging up on statistics and other technical issues. No longer could the department simply announce plans and expect to see them quietly come to fruition. Mick Hamer describes in his book on the roads lobby how a meeting in Shipley Town Hall about the Aire Valley motorway, the M650 (the three digits rather give away the fact that it was solving a traffic problem that did not exist), was disrupted when

> two chairs which had been jamming the door handles splintered and fell away. In rushed an angry crowd led by a local

> farmer... Suddenly, through the doors of Shipley Town Hall
> flooded a tide of people who had gained the self-confidence
> to challenge the unchallengeable. No longer were they to be
> fobbed off by technicalities, or defeated by rules that loaded
> the dice in the ministry's favour.[14]

The inquiry was abandoned and the road never built.

The road lobby, however, had not gone away, and there were repeated attempts to kick-start a major programme of road building. In London a series of four assessment studies were published in the late 1980s looking at ways of bringing dual carriageways and motorways further into the centre, but fervent opposition and awareness of the high cost meant they came to nothing. With the exception of the M11 Link and a few minor schemes, building new roads in London was now untenable. Margaret Thatcher, ever keen on helping the motorist, published a White Paper, 'Roads for prosperity', which set out 'the biggest road building programme for the UK since the Romans'. (Politicians love these fatuous claims – every announcement of rail investment is 'the biggest since Victorian times'.) While parts of it, such as motorway widening, have gone ahead, much of it was never started because of opposition not just from hippy road protesters like the famous Swampy, who lived in a threatened forest for a time and ended up briefly writing a column for the *Daily Mirror*, but also from Conservative blue-rinse ladies in rural areas that would have been affected.

In fact, oddly, it was a victory that did most damage to the road lobby cause. The government had proposed a cutting through Twyford Down, a beauty spot in Hampshire, near the South Downs National Park as part of the M3 to replace the Winchester bypass. After furious protests, which turned violent at times, the road was completed but the environmental damage it has caused, effectively destroying a small hill and a plateau of grasslands, is all too obvious for miles around. The battle of Twyford Down may have been lost, but in many respects the war against further massive road

Twyford Down cutting.
Source: photo by Jim Champion (see page 115 for full details).

building was won there. Any roads protester only has to point to a photograph of the Twyford Down cutting, with the lovely landscape scarred permanently by a stream of cars and lorries, to destroy any ministerial promises that a particular scheme will not be as damaging as protesters claim.

Following the completion of this section of the M3, the Conservative government, which at the time of the Twyford protests argued that it was planting lots of trees to mitigate the impact of new roads, became reluctant to push ahead with further schemes as damaging as Twyford Down. Indeed, the intellectual underpinning of the roads programme was severely damaged by the publication of a report in 1994 by the obscure but influential Standing Advisory Committee on Trunk Road Assessment (SACTRA). The report found that there was strong evidence that new roads attracted more vehicles onto them. The M25, completed in 1986, reached the traffic flows predicted for 2000 in just eighteen months. In other words, by providing extra road capacity, more journeys, and consequently more traffic, were generated. This greatly undermined the case for new roads because it distorted the cost–benefit ratio analysis. That is because the benefits, in terms of journey time savings, are exaggerated, since if some of the journeys would not have taken place without the new infrastructure, then it is a fundamental error to argue that time savings are made as a consequence. As the SACTRA team concluded:

> These studies demonstrate convincingly that the economic value of a scheme can be overestimated by the omission of even a small amount of induced traffic. We consider that this matter is of profound importance to the value for money assessment of the Road Programme.[15]

In other words, the way roads were valued in the methodology used by the Department of Transport was fundamentally flawed.

By and large it began to be accepted that the era of major new roads was over. The motorway network was essentially considered complete, apart from the odd link, and while a few bypasses or schemes to sort out junctions were still being built, most subsequent additions to the system have been 'improvements', which usually means widening or adding lanes. New roads in urban areas, which required demolition of buildings, were no longer being proposed.

And this is where there has been the most fundamental failure. Although it has been recognized that it is no longer possible to add capacity – we are not going to get the sixteen-lane highways of Los Angeles or Beijing – the obvious policy responses are either to constrain demand by encouraging alternative modes of transport or to charge for what is an economic 'good' that is in short supply.

Let the train take the strain – or not?

However, the subsequent policy response to the opposition to roads and to the findings of SACTRA has been muddled, to say the least, and often contradictory. The obvious environmental, economic and social requirement to reduce road traffic has, at times, been a stated aim of government, but it has always been expressed in the context of not wanting to affect motorists. Crucially, no clear common intellectual thread can be detected from the subsequent vagaries of transport policy that has been buffeted by external forces. It is the failure to learn from history and develop a coherent way forward that has characterized successive regimes at the Department for Transport.

Throughout the period when the emphasis of transport policy was on trying to provide for the car, the other modes were in decline. Without any coherent transport strategy or any proper understanding of the limitations of untrammelled motorization, the policies on the railways were muddled and incoherent. In the interwar period, the rail industry was under the control of four private companies, which were the result of an enforced amalgamation when the railways were returned to the private sector in the aftermath of World War I. Facing competition from the lorry, the coach and later the private car, and hamstrung by tight government regulations that forced them to be 'common carriers' (that is, they were forced to transport any load offered to them, including circuses and farm removals), none of them were particularly profitable. This meant that their ability to invest and to respond to changing market conditions was constrained, although there were some successes, such as the much-improved expresses on the lucrative London–Scotland routes and the electrification of most routes on the Southern Railway, which not only sped up services but also increased capacity and reduced costs.

After World War II, when the railways were again temporarily nationalized, the Labour government decided to take them permanently into state ownership, where they remained for nearly fifty years. Initially after nationalization they were starved of funds, having to compete with the huge investment needs of post-war Britain. Then something surprising happened. The Conservative government of the mid 1950s decided to modernize the railways, not because they were particularly supportive of them but rather because they perceived them as being important to industry. Given that times were still tough, it was a remarkable move: the cost was £1.24 billion (around £26 billion in 2016 prices) and the importance of the railways, in the face of rising car ownership and increasing road haulage, was declining. The plan used a scattergun approach, attempting to modernize all aspects of the industry, and focused very much on capital schemes: thirty huge new marshalling yards, at a time when wagon load freight was seeing the most rapid decline; shiny new locomotives (174 different types of diesel locomotives were to be tested to find the best ones); and enhancements to tracks, such as a flyover at Bletchley that was never used because connecting lines were closed. Electrification of the West Coast Main Line and various London commuter routes were probably its most useful contribution, but much money was wasted. Most importantly, the idea that this once-and-for-all boost to the railways would ensure that it could then become profitable was a pipe dream. Railways, as I have mentioned before, stubbornly refuse to play the conventional economic game of making a return on capital.

The failure of the 'Modernisation Plan' led to a complete U-turn in relation to the railways. Suddenly, with Ernest Marples installed as transport minister in 1959, the solution was to cut back the dead wood on the railways: a task carried out – under orders – by the infamous Richard Beeching.

In his report 'The reshaping of British railways', published in 1963, Beeching stressed that the railways were a very unbalanced network. A quarter of fare income came from just thirty-four stations (approximately 0.5% of the total), while at the other end of the scale half of the remaining stations produced just 2% of passenger income. Critics of Beeching's approach have pointed out that this was a dishonest way of assessing the industry. David Henshaw, author of a critical assessment of Beeching's legacy, suggests a similar examination of roads would reveal a similar imbalance:

> The vast majority of minor roads would have been deemed uneconomic. The density of road traffic was spread just as unevenly as rail traffic.[16]

It is a telling point, and illustrative of a key failing of thinking on transport policy throughout the modern era.

Beeching's terms of reference, which were to find a way of returning the industry to profitability as soon as possible, were such that his recommendations were inevitable. His report envisaged a huge programme of retrenchment, with the result that 2,363 stations (more than half the total number) and 5,000 miles of line (just under a third) were closed. What was less inevitable was the enthusiasm with which the Labour government, elected in October 1964 partly on a manifesto promise to halt the closures, set about implementing Beeching's proposals, even shutting some lines that had not been earmarked in the report.

Of course many of these closures were justified but they were carried out without any clear strategy about what the rail industry was for, and were instead purely focused on making the railways profitable. In the event, Beeching's savings were of the order of £30 million annually, while losses were more than three times that level – these figures are not definitive, though, because of the opaque nature of British Rail accounting methods.

The Labour government of the late sixties did, however, recognize the need for a more systematic approach to rail policy. The result was Barbara Castle's 1968 Transport Act, which, for the first time, acknowledged that the railways needed financial support from the government to maintain lines that were socially useful. This created a distinction between loss-making and profitable lines. Closures slowed to a trickle after the 1968 Act and stopped completely by 1977, and since then only the odd redundant mile or two has been shut and there have been no threats of major closures. In fact, quite the opposite. More than 500 miles of railway and 370 stations have been reopened in the past fifty years, and there are many campaigns across the country seeking more.

The lack of closures was not, though, for want of trying by significant groups of British Rail managers and civil servants in the 1970s and 1980s. In their two recent books *Holding the Line* and *Disconnected!*, Chris Austin and Richard (Lord) Faulkner have uncovered a series of attempts to undermine the railways and make major cuts to the network in the thirty-year period between the Beeching era and privatization. Most shockingly, a secret conference of civil servants and politicians was held, without British Rail's knowledge, in Sunningdale in 1977 with the explicit aim of drawing up a massive closure programme. There was also the Serpell Report, published in 1982, in which one option suggested cutting back the whole network to a rump of 1,600 miles (out of

10,000), but this was killed off rapidly after British Rail pre-empted its publication with a judicious leak. The last throes of the 'shut it down' brigade was the attempt in the late 1980s to close the Settle–Carlisle railway on the spurious grounds that it was too expensive to maintain – a plan that was eventually killed off by a spirited campaign by local opponents and the arrival of Michael Portillo, later to become a true rail buff, at the Department of Transport in 1988. Faulkner and Austin summarize the period by suggesting that, while the build-up to the Beeching report is well known,

> what is remarkable – and shocking – is the discovery of just how determined the railway managers and civil servants of particularly the 1970s, and also the 1980s, were to reduce the size of the network with which they were entrusted, even after public opinion had turned against major closures, and politicians had wisely followed them.[17]

Again, this demonstrates the incoherence of government policies on the railways and on transport in general. While there was seemingly, at last, a recognition of the social value of trains, the policy as put forward by the department never seemed to fully reflect that.

The privatization of the railways in the 1990s has only added to the confusion over their role. The ideologues behind the sale thought that selling off the railways would not only result in their becoming profitable – thereby obviating the need for any subsidy – but would also enable the government to withdraw from responsibility for their operation. Both notions proved to be incorrect. The railways still receive around £3.5 billion per year in subsidy, largely to fund investment but also to support loss-making services, and government is as involved as ever, partly because of the need for subsidy but also because the railways are a key part of the nation's infrastructure.

Today, there is at least a recognition of their value. Indeed, just as building new roads has become very difficult in the current climate of public opinion, closing rail lines is also politically impossible. The railways have cross-party support and investing in them is now seen as axiomatic for the growth of the economy. All three main parties support the construction of HS2, a £50 billion project to build 335 miles of high-speed line linking London with Birmingham, Manchester and Leeds, and the railways have a £38.5 billion investment programme covering the five years from April 2014, which involves major sections of electrification. However, it has proved difficult for the state-owned Network Rail to deliver this investment programme, and there are suggestions that it may need to be reined back. Nevertheless, there remains unprecedented across-the-board support for the railways.

No bus to hop on

Until 1930, the bus and coach industry was unregulated. Motor buses, which had started operating in the first decade of the 1900s, became universal after World War I when numerous small bus companies were started by ex-servicemen. There was intense competition in many towns and cities but less so in London, where the London General Omnibus Company had achieved a measure of dominance. The major companies – Thomas Tilling, British Electric Traction (a bus company despite the name) and National – gradually took over many smaller concerns, and the Road Traffic Act 1930, which introduced regulation into the industry, resulted in further consolidation. London's bus service, which stretched thirty miles out from the centre with its Green Line coach routes, was effectively nationalized and run as part of the enormous newly created London Transport.

After World War II, the state-owned British Transport Commission acquired most of the bus companies. There was not, as was the case with the railways, a forced nationalization but – with both central and local government keen to preserve services in the face of the decline in passenger numbers resulting from greater car use – by the late 1960s most services were either state or local-authority owned. The 1968 Transport Act formalized the position, creating the National Bus Company to run all local bus services in England and Wales except those in London and in five major conurbations where services were under the control of newly created Passenger Transport Executives.

The need for ever-increasing subsidies, as passenger numbers continued to decline, and the dislike of state-owned enterprises led Margaret Thatcher to break up the National Bus Company and open services up to competition through the 1985 Transport Act. Famously, the transport minister of the time, Nicholas Ridley, had the notion that individual bus drivers could buy their own vehicle and operate it themselves. He was wont, when touring bus garages, to suggest precisely that to rather bemused drivers. The deregulation did not work out like that. While for a few years there were bus wars on lucrative high street routes in several towns and cities, which often attracted negative publicity (and some of the buses appeared to date back to World War II), five major bus groups quite rapidly emerged, and they tended not to compete with each other as they had tacit agreement not to encroach on each other's territory. A handful of municipally owned companies, notably in Reading and Nottingham, managed to stave off the blandishments of the major groups and survive. The emphasis in the main, however, was on competition. Anyone with an operator's licence could start a bus service with just six weeks' notice, and with very few requirements other than safety measures being met. Even the radical Tory government remained too wary to allow a free-for-all in London, where services remain regulated, operated under management contracts set by

Transport for London, which determines the routes and frequency and retains all the fare income.

Despite thirteen years of Labour government, and much pressure from various local politicians, Labour did not re-regulate the provincial bus services. It created the potential for 'Quality Contracts', which would have placed greater social obligations on the private companies, but it made it so difficult for local authorities to implement the policy, with massive safeguards for the private operators, that none did so.

Consequently, in most towns and cities, the private operators run the profitable routes but, unlike under the old municipalized system, no longer cross-subsidize the loss-making services in the network. Consequently, these are tendered out by local councils, who have to make up the shortfall in income – something they are finding increasingly difficult to do. It is in sharp contrast to many European cities where whole systems are franchised out, in much the same way as in London, thereby ensuring that the network is specified by the public authority. The bus companies argue that this stymies commercial innovation and market responsiveness, but, as the surviving municipally owned bus companies show by frequently winning awards at industry events, they are often able to combine good service with commercial acumen.

In one of those bizarre political twists, the Conservative government that was elected in 2015 appears to be prepared to allow some local authorities the freedom to control bus services in their areas providing they agree to a package of measures, including the election of an executive mayor, to devolve power. Manchester was the first area to benefit from this policy, but there have been moves to expand it to several others, including Cornwall.

Where are those trams?

After becoming less fashionable than bloomers and plus fours, trams eventually began to again be recognized as a very effective form of urban transport. France led the way in Europe, with new tram systems in Grenoble and Nantes in the mid 1980s, and even in car-dominated North America systems began appearing in places as diverse as Calgary, Portland and San Diego. Britain was slow off the mark, opening its first schemes in Manchester and Sheffield in 1992. London got its only tramline, the Croydon Tramlink, in 2000, and so far, if the historic Blackpool system (which has now been given new rolling stock) is included, eight urban areas can now boast systems. The latest one is in Edinburgh, where the massive cost overruns and delays have probably killed off any hopes of new systems being built for a generation. There are also the Tyne and Wear Metro (1980) and London's Docklands Light Railway (1987), which are classified as light rail though unlike trams they do not run on roads, but again this is a story of missed opportunities. Most of the new British systems, particularly those in Croydon, Manchester and Nottingham, have been successful and well patronized. The Nottingham system benefited from finance generated by a workplace parking levy – the only such scheme in the country but one that clearly has the potential to provide funding for other new transport infrastructure.

Nottingham tram.
Source: photo by Malc McDonald (see page 115 for full details).

France, for example, which closed all its systems in the post-war period, now has twenty-seven networks, including in modest-sized cities such as Valenciennes (population just 43,000) and Caen (109,000), the equivalent of cities such as Grantham (population 41,000 – but a tram network would surely send Margaret Thatcher spinning in her grave) and Stroud (population 115,000) being blessed with trams.

In the UK, John Prescott, when he was transport secretary, did try. He published a transport plan in 2000 that suggested twenty-five tram lines would be built across the country by 2010, paid for partly by road pricing in many towns and cities. Neither the road pricing, apart from in London, nor the tram schemes, with the exception of the one in Nottingham, saw the light of day by the proposed date of 2010, nor in fact by 2016. This failure was partly due to the fact that Prescott's genuine enthusiasm and support for the idea was not matched by his colleagues round the Cabinet table. Transport was seen as being of minor interest but, worse, other ministers were terrified of the negative effects of raising the cost of motoring. The launch of a White Paper in the summer of 2000 coincided with a series of protests by truck drivers over the increasing cost of fuel. Although Chancellor Gordon Brown's policy of a fuel tax escalator had by then been abandoned, more than 80% of the cost of fuel was tax and the truckers took action by blockading several refineries. While they relented before any serious shortages developed, the fear that they would rise up again was to colour future transport policy.

Moreover, in France and most other European countries, local authorities, which are often very keen on big transport innovations such as light rail, are able to draw up plans and drive them through, usually with some support from central government. In the UK, by contrast, local government is weak both financially and administratively, which means that the initiative for such projects has to come from central government, where the *zeitgeist* can change all too quickly.

In an email he sent to me, Oliver Green, the author of *Rails in the Road: A History of Tramways in Britain and Ireland*, explains how it has proved impossible to get a scheme off the ground in his home town:

> In Oxford trams could have a major impact on the horrendous traffic problems both of Oxford City and the surrounding county, and could be linked to branch rail lines to Cowley and Witney to relieve the congested main A40 into Oxford. The problem is that City and County never cooperate (political opposites) and neither of them work properly with Network Rail or the Highways Agency to coordinate plans. We seem to be obsessed in the UK with doing everything as cheaply as possible, so at the moment the best our local authorities can come up with are bus lanes and more park-and-ride schemes which will not be adequate.

The failure of Prescott's plan was, in fact, more fundamental: it was not just about tram schemes but was a missed opportunity in what could have been a seminal moment in British transport history, changing the course of transport policy. The ideas in the plan were in fact based, in somewhat watered down form, on the radical thinking of Professor Phil Goodwin, an adviser to John Prescott who had also been influential on the committee that produced the 1994 SACTRA report discussed earlier. Goodwin had, it seemed, managed to finally persuade the government that what he called a 'New Realism' was required, a rejection of the idea that transport problems would be solved by building new roads. He later told the BBC:

> a lot of people associated with the rethinking of transport policy felt the same thing ... a feeling that yes, this was the first time maybe that professionals and politicians were seeing eye to eye.[18]

However, Prescott lost his hands-on role in the Department for Transport in 2001, and it was the arrival there of Alistair Darling the following year that killed off most of Prescott's cherished schemes. Darling was keener on balancing the books than on leaving anything to posterity. He was to be in post for four years and made it his duty to ensure that virtually no significant transport schemes were given the go-ahead, apart from measures to improve safety on the railways after the series of accidents in the aftermath of privatization.

The only subsequent attempt to create a national transport strategy or plan also came to naught. The Eddington Report on Britain's infrastructure needs

– commissioned by Darling when he finally bowed to pressure to have something to show for his tenure at transport – was published in 2006. However, whether by accident or design, Darling had chosen the right person to ensure that nothing much would result. Rather than advocating a series of massive new investments and additions to the network (as had been widely expected by people within the transport industry), the author, Rod Eddington, who had been an aviation executive, broadly concluded that transport links within the UK were pretty good and there was no need for a network of high-speed lines or major improvements to the road system. He did, however, predictably want to see expanded airport capacity and better links to ports. In order to help congestion in overcrowded cities and on key inter-urban routes, he advocated the gradual introduction of a road-pricing scheme – something that politicians have never dared to put forward because of fears of widespread opposition. Like Prescott's effort and previous 'we must do something' efforts at the department, Eddington's report was allowed to gather dust on a Whitehall shelf and is rarely referred to today.

Chapter 5

Is technology the answer?

The current transport situation was reached because of an obsession with a mode of transport that provides great benefit to the individual at a cost to wider society, in conjunction with a failure to recognize the value of collective forms of transport, despite their proven value.

Rather than addressing the fundamental imbalance in transport policy, policymakers often dodge the issue by looking to technological development as the solution. The starting point, however, must be to ask: if technology is the answer, what is the question? What are we trying to achieve? What, therefore, are the major transport problems that technology could and should be addressing?

The problems can be set out in two broad categories. The first is the inadequacies of the system. In other words, the fact that it is in many instances difficult to get from A to B, whether through lack of infrastructure, poor services or excess demand. The second category concerns the negative effects of transport, such as accidents, air pollution, energy consumption, environmental degradation and, again, excess demand causing congestion and overcrowding.

When it comes to the first category above, there is no doubt that technology can be very useful in numerous ways. There is no shortage of examples. The installation of digital information at bus stops to show when the next service is arriving has made bus travel far more efficient – enabling people to make choices about whether to wait or use an alternative mode of transport. The provision of hire bikes in many city centres has been made possible by technology that monitors when they are taken out of their stands and returned to them. Technology has also greatly improved the ease with which people can take public transport. No longer do passengers have to queue up at ticket offices: they can open the gates and access the system using their smart cards (such as Oyster in London) or simply with a contactless bank card. Big data is proving invaluable in improving traffic flow on city streets, with every vehicle now becoming a source of information, and the ever-growing sophistication of traffic light systems contributes to reducing congestion.

Uber is probably the most interesting example of a use of technology in the transport field that superficially appears to offer only enormous benefits but that, as we drill down to consider its effects, creates major problems, too. On the face of it, what's not to like? Uber offers the chance to call cabs via an app wherever you are (and you can use the same app in Birmingham, Berlin or Beirut) and then your fare is paid via the internet, obviating the need to fiddle with change (and probably tip) – and normally, except at times of very high demand, at a far lower cost than conventional cabs. The driver will be known to Uber, and passengers are able to rate the experience, ensuring that there is a high standard of service. (Hopefully, the driver who told a woman passenger in a miniskirt that she was inappropriately dressed was not allowed to remain on Uber's books!)

However, the investors in Uber are not interested in the provision of a better service for urban taxi users. They are concerned only with making a profit, and doing so involves disrupting the existing taxi industry. There is no doubt that in many major cities restrictive practices designed to regulate the industry – but also protect its drivers, who are often a powerful local lobbying force – have meant higher charges than the free market would deliver. They also have meant, certainly in London, the guarantee of a quality product with high safety standards and relatively good customer care (though when I watch, as I frequently do, taxi drivers sitting on their butts with their engines running at St Pancras while tourists struggle to load their suitcases into their cabs, I do accept that the industry could do with a bit of a shake-up). The requirement in London for a prospective cabbie to take 'the Knowledge', which generally takes a couple of years, is a way of limiting newcomers to the business and has pretty much been made redundant by the introduction of satnavs. However, Uber threatens to do much more than simply give the existing taxi industry a somewhat deserved kick in the rear end. Its aim, ultimately, is the complete disintegration of institutions like the black cab trade.

Because the rules governing the influx of new private hire drivers, the definition that covers Uber, are so lax, Transport for London does not have the ability to control numbers. The technology that has allowed the creation of Uber has therefore led to a sharp increase in traffic in central London as Uber drivers, who are exempt from the congestion charge, hang about, like prostitutes in Amsterdam doorways, waiting for business and cluttering up the streets, reversing a trend that has seen traffic in central London steadily decline or remain static in most of the years since the introduction of the congestion charge in 2003. So while Uber may have brought down fares somewhat, it has also caused major disruption. And if the taxi trade were to be wiped out by the newcomer, would those fares remain low?

None of these examples represents a transport revolution. Much of the recent technological development is about making systems more efficient, rather than creating totally new forms of mobility. Ticket offices can be closed, toll booths can be eliminated and traffic lights can operate more efficiently. Sure, one benefit of new technology is that it enables the implementation of ideas that would otherwise not be economically feasible. A bike hire system on the scale of the London Santander Cycles scheme could not be provided like a left luggage office of the 1950s, with cap-doffing men issuing bikes from a back office and collecting them back with complaints about scratches! (It is interesting that, for the most part, hire cars are still issued in this way, though the Paris Autolib' system is changing this, as are various initiatives such as Zipcar in the UK and elsewhere.) At the end of the day, though, it is simply a way of loaning out bikes to people in the way that late Victorians did in public parks. Knowing when the next bus is coming is hardly rocket science either. I remember being in Oakland, California in the early 1970s and simply ringing up to find out when the next bus was arriving before leaving the house in which I was staying – and that was perfectly reliable.

Largely, then, it is not technology that drives change – instead, it is the other way round: change demands technological developments that then become financially viable. The notion that technology is developing far faster now than ever before, and therefore will engender far-reaching changes, is misplaced. The inventions of the nineteenth and early twentieth centuries were the real mould-breakers. Before the railways, no one had travelled faster than a horse could gallop, and the development of the telegraph and, later, the telephone similarly sped up communication, which had previously relied on four-legged animals, to the speed of light. Electricity improved people's lives in rather more fundamental ways than the mobile telephone has.

Nowhere is this more marked than in the discussion of driverless (or, rather, robot) cars, which have attracted massive media attention and have been presented as a solution to today's transport problems. Yet any considered examination of their potential suggests they will create just as many new problems as they will solve. In particular, they do not address the fundamental issue of the shortage of road space, nor of the environmental degradation caused by existing vehicles – not only pollution but the land use taken up by roads and parking.

The driverless car: a game changer?
Source: photo by Grendelkhan (see page 115 for full details).

Even if cars used no energy and created no polluting gases, they would still be a blight on urban areas.

In any case, despite the billions being invested in them, robot cars so far remain a highly experimental concept that is nowhere near coming to fruition in any meaningful way. While aspects of driverless cars such as cruise control and automatic parking have been introduced to today's car fleet, the technology of allowing autonomous control of a car while the driver sits and reads her copy of the *Financial Times* or plays with his tablet is nowhere near ready.

Google cars have driven more than a million miles around California, but in very restricted conditions and limited to twenty-five miles per hour. That compares with some three trillion miles driven annually in the United States. Moreover, they are only able to be controlled automatically in good conditions: 'the current prototypes of self-driving vehicles cannot yet operate safely in fog, snow, or heavy rain', according to the University of Michigan Transportation Research Institute.[19] While better sensors may overcome these problems – researchers suggest that heavy rain is the most difficult of these to overcome – there are doubts about whether the cars will be able to cope with more extreme events, such as a flooded road or a power line that has fallen on the roadway. Talk, therefore, of widespread introduction within a decade or so, which some promoters are suggesting, seems fanciful or even downright impossible.

Moreover, they have had a disproportionately high number of crashes, albeit minor ones. The cars in California had accumulated eleven such accidents by the middle of 2015, and in February 2016 a prang with a bus was actually caused by the 'driverless car'. While the earlier incidents were not the fault of the automation, it may be that human drivers find the behaviour of driverless cars less predictable. Most of these accidents were rear-end shunts and the excessive caution of the robot cars is thought to have been a contributory cause. They slowed down or stopped in a situation that the driver behind did not perceive as being dangerous.

This demonstrates possibly the biggest difficulty that robot cars would face in emulating human driving conditions. Consider, for example, how drivers pull out of side roads into busy but relatively slow-moving roads – they inch out, creep and eventually some kind-hearted driver slows down to let them out, something that is much easier in the UK than in many other countries. Think of the number of human interactions that take place between drivers and the skill needed to ensure that the car in the side road inches out just enough to induce someone to let them through but not so much that an accident is caused.

This is in fact precisely the sort of event that occurred in the first accident caused by the 'driverless car'. The incident report is very revealing in that it demonstrates the extent to which the 'driverless car' is nothing of the sort as the test driver is expected to make key decisions. The Google car was attempting to turn right at traffic lights (on red, which is allowed in the US) and had got into a bit of a tangle with some sandbags, forcing it back into the middle of the road. The report then says:

> A public transit bus was approaching from behind. The Google AV [automatic vehicle] test driver saw the bus approaching in the left side mirror *but believed the bus would stop or slow to allow the Google AV to continue.*

The italics are mine, and they are there to highlight the fact that test drivers clearly make many decisions on the way that the cars are driven. The bus did not stop, and it hit the slow-moving Google car at around fifteen miles per hour, causing extensive damage but no injury.

This incident clearly illustrates the dilemma about 'driverless cars': they will be expected, eventually, to take risks and that will inevitably result in them causing some accidents, with all the issues that that entails. The four-way stop sign, greatly favoured in residential areas in America, could easily turn out to be a permanent bottleneck with robot cars. The programmers are now thinking of creating software that would enable the cars to break the safety rules to allow for these situations but this could, by definition, cause an accident that was the robot car's fault. It may be a catch-22 too far for their developers.

There is an assumption among many advocates of driverless cars that they would become some kind of communal resource, rather like the Santander bikes in London, because they would reduce the need or desire for individual ownership. But there is no evidence for that. The 'keeping up with the Joneses' aspect of car ownership may be weakening, as cars all look the same and seem to be predominantly black or silver, but it still remains, as attested to by the ridiculous number of Chelsea tractors, not just in Chelsea but throughout London. The twin revolution of driverless cars and common ownership may well prove to be a myth, or at least not deliverable in the sort of time frame that would allow today's policymakers to consider it.

The key issue is whether driverless cars will result in an increase or a reduction in mileage. If driverless cars live up to their promise, it appears logical that they would attract people out of public transport given their flexibility and the fact that they provide private space – all the current attractions of driving without the need to waste time controlling the damn thing. Driverless cars may well, then, replicate the failed transport policies of the past and exacerbate, rather than solve, the fundamental problem of the commons, i.e. the overuse of communal road space that is provided free. We have been here before. The motor car was originally sold as a panacea to transportation problems. How much easier, its promoters said, it made getting from one's current location to precisely where one wanted to be. However, that only worked for a while. Once cars became more widely used, sheer numbers of vehicles and parking restrictions made that impossible. Many people still think that having a (free) parking space outside their front door is a fundamental human right but, especially in the urban context, fewer and fewer are able to enjoy that luxury.

The same doubts about the game-changing nature of technology applies to driverless trains or other developments on the railways, such as moving block signalling, which means that trains are no longer controlled by external signals but by radio waves sent into the cab to ensure they maintain a safe distance from the train in front. While this may result in more trains being able to use the tracks, the nineteenth-century technology of rails on sleepers still prevails and is the limiting factor. The cost of providing extra tracks remains prohibitive and is the biggest barrier to expanding the system.

Electric cars are another technology that flatters to deceive. There is a wide variety of technologies, ranging from hybrid to pure electric vehicles. Hybrids clearly only offer partial environmental benefits, and even electric cars, until they are powered by sustainable methods, still create CO_2 emissions. Despite the fact that fully electric vehicles offer considerable advantages to the consumer, with far cheaper fuel, and to society at large, with lower emissions, uptake of electric vehicles has been slow, even in Paris where there are lots of recharging facilities – the main advantage of which has been to provide free parking for users!

The purchase price of electric cars remains far higher than for conventional cars, despite government grants, and concerns about driving range, given the paucity of charging points, are a limiting factor to their use. The cost of new batteries remains high and though there are now some deals that involve simply leasing the battery, reducing the risk to the driver, the overall cost still has to be paid for by the user. In addition, electric vehicles will only contribute significantly to the reduction of greenhouse gases if the power they use is generated sustainably. The European Union wants 20% of energy to come from renewable sources by 2020, a target that the UK will struggle to reach given the changes to subsidy arrangements brought in by the government soon after the 2015 election.

Technology, therefore, has to be the tool of the transport planners, not their master. Some of these ideas may be partial solutions or at least alleviate problems, but they do not address the fundamental complexity of transport issues. Policymakers have at times been lured by visions of the future that seem to be a panacea. I remember those pictures from the 1960s of people being propelled by backpack rockets or sitting in tiny little aircraft that would get them to work. More significantly and prosaically, the Buchanan concept of separating cars from pedestrians was actually implemented in places as diverse as Birmingham and the Barbican. The hard truth is that there is no silver bullet that will simultaneously solve the downsides of transport: congestion, pollution and energy use.

Chapter 6

Can't we build ourselves out of trouble?

Transport policy has for decades been driven on the basis of 'predict and provide'. There is going to be more demand for road space, so build it – or at least try to. Policymakers have been able to do this because transport is seen as a public good. In other words, the norms of capitalist provision, of meeting supply and demand, do not apply. Public goods can supposedly be consumed by people without detriment to others seeking the same service. That is the theory. But in practice, as we have seen, that does not work, because ultimately supply has to be limited. It is probably in China where the authorities have gone furthest in trying to prove that it is possible to keep on feeding demand, and even there they seem to have given up as attempts to build a seventh ring road around Beijing are now being abandoned.

In the UK, predict and provide was the prevailing ethos in relation to car use pretty much from the end of World War I until the cost and contradictions of the policy came home to roost towards the end of the twentieth century. Aviation policy, too, has largely been determined by the predict-and-provide ethos and, given the growth in railway passengers, it is now being applied to the rail industry, though the lumpiness and cost of investment is a deterrent.

While there has been increasing scepticism about basing transport policy on such a simplistic notion, weaning transport planners and policymakers away from it has proved difficult. This is partly a consequence of the widespread use of cost–benefit analysis, the dominant methodology for calculating the advantages of new transport schemes. The basic notion is sound: when considering whether or not to build a scheme, the promoters are required to set out the benefits and costs that will result. So far, so good. The costs of a scheme are fairly obvious: the direct spending required to build it and an assessment of indirect costs, such as, for example, noise pollution or environmental degradation. However, it is the nature of the benefits that is far more controversial. The methodology used by the Department for Transport (called WebTag) relies very heavily, for most schemes, on time savings made by users of the new infrastructure. These are then monetized, averaging around £25 per hour per person but varying considerably depending on the mode of transport of the user and the reason for travelling, with business travellers being rated more highly than those undertaking leisure trips. These time savings make up a very high proportion of the savings for most schemes, and these savings in turn become the core of the business case on which the Department for Transport and consequently politicians rely in order to sell their plans to the public.

However, the figures produced by this method have little relationship to reality. It is fanciful to assume that small time savings – often, in the case of a bypass or minor road scheme, amounting to just a minute or less per person – represent real value to the economy. In one of the most farcical attempts to justify a transport policy on this basis, in a 2011 Department for Transport press release, Philip Hammond (then the Transport Secretary) claimed that increasing the speed limit on motorways from seventy to eighty miles per hour 'could provide hundreds of millions of pounds of benefits for the economy' because people would get to their destinations slightly faster (he omitted to mention the fact that there would be more accidents, resulting in additional delays).

In fact, cost–benefit analysis was never originally intended to demonstrate whether a scheme was worthwhile but, rather, was meant to be a fairly rough-and-ready method for comparing different projects. It was first used widely in the 1960s in order to give planners a way of convincing politicians that they should sanction schemes but it has become an indispensable tool for the promoters of any transport project, even very small ones such as altering a junction layout. Now, cost–benefit analysis has turned into a massive consultant bonanza that purports to give very precise figures for the future value of a scheme over, say, thirty years by rolling up annual benefits to provide an estimate of the project's present value. We therefore get ridiculous headlines in the media saying that a particular transport project will be worth £10 billion or £100 billion to the economy over the next thirty years. This has as much accuracy as predicting how many pigeons will land on Hyde Park next month, and yet the whole of transport policy is geared towards the approval and delivery of schemes that deliver the best benefit–cost ratio. This tends to favour bigger schemes as the benefits can be presented as very large, and also results in ignoring schemes that deliver benefits other than time savings.

Indeed, the lack of infrastructure in the UK can be put down to an obsession with the narrow assessment of their value in terms of business cases that fail to take into account a whole raft of wider considerations. The obsession with producing a precise number for the long-term value of a scheme, based on the methodology of cost–benefit assessments, has been highly damaging in both stopping very useful schemes from being built and encouraging others, notably roads, that should not.

No cure for the roads addiction

The roads programme has not been subject to the same political vagaries as the railways. There was never a Beeching of the roads, even though the same kind of statistics about how most of them are little used could be applied. There have been ups and downs in the investment programme, certainly, but by and large few politicians dare speak ill of the 'need' for better roads.

The Labour government of 1997–2010 reined back on the new roads programme, in line with the scepticism about predict and provide. However, the coalition government that succeeded it began, once again, to talk up road investment, culminating in a promise in November 2014 by the Chancellor, George Osborne, to spend £15 billion on new schemes over the ensuing five years. Ministers, as mentioned previously, are keen on stressing they are implementing the biggest road building programme since the Romans but in fact, nowadays, road investment is largely about incremental addition: a short link to avoid a bottleneck, say, or the addition of a lane.

The basis of the large road building programme, however, even on a predict and provide model, is weak. Despite the increase in car registrations, the number of miles travelled by cars has remained virtually unchanged from the turn of the century until very recently, when there has been a small upturn. The Department for

Transport, however, predicts that there will be strong growth in the next two decades even on a model based on increasing fuel prices. The situation is therefore somewhat muddled. The low cost of fuel may well have resulted in some short-term increase but predictions of a significant rise in mileage are much more uncertain. The greater use of new forms of communication such as video conferencing, the increased potential to work at home afforded by broadband, the reluctance of young people to buy cars and drive, and even developments such as the miniaturization of electronic goods may all mitigate against increased demand for road space. However, information technology can work both ways, reducing the propensity to travel for, say, meetings, but also encouraging travel by increasing connectivity. The increase in popularity of living in town centres, where car ownership tends to be lower, is another factor that may account for reduced demand, since luxury flats can be sold in central London without car parking spaces. Moreover, it is highly likely that politicians will eventually be forced into considering road pricing given the reduced revenue from fuel tax as cars increase in efficiency and the use of electric and hybrid vehicles increases.

Nevertheless, the default position of politicians on transport policy when predictions of increased demand are made remains to launch further expansion of road capacity. Since, as argued previously, it is almost impossible to increase capacity in urban areas because of opposition, the roads programme is oriented towards inter-urban and regional transport, which is not where there is serious congestion on the network.

While investment in trunk roads has continued apace, the same is not true of local roads, where spending has suffered severe cuts in recent times. All but 5% of roads are managed by local authorities, and those authorities have been subject to a series of cuts that, by 2015, had left them with a shortfall of £8.6 billion (according to the Local Government Association). While such figures need to be taken with a pinch of salt, there is evidence that the condition of roads is deteriorating throughout the country. A report by the RAC Foundation called 'The condition of England's local roads and how they are funded' suggested that 4% of A roads and 8% of B and C roads are in need of maintenance work and that an estimated 2.5 million potholes need filling annually. The government periodically announces special funds to fix potholes but has traditionally been more ready to support road construction rather than routine maintenance.

The strange case of HS2

When politicians are intent on doing something, their own, supposedly evidence-based, approach goes out of the window. The lure of being remembered for a scheme is sometimes too tempting, even if by the time ribbons are cut they will be long gone. That is the only possible explanation for the cross-party support for HS2, the high-speed railway that will link London with Birmingham, Manchester and Leeds. The business case in terms of the benefit–cost ratio is incredibly tenuous for such a massive scheme given the huge proportion of the transport budget it will take up: including rolling stock, the cost is expected to be £50 billion (including some contingency or optimum bias), a figure that is widely expected to increase.

Yet the momentum behind the HS2 scheme appears to make it unstoppable. Already some £1 billion has been spent on it and there is all-party support. Despite the cost and deep cuts to government spending, George Osborne sees it as the centrepiece of his Northern Powerhouse and, more generally, of his desire to improve Britain's infrastructure.

It is quite difficult to unpick precisely how HS2 has become all but a fait accompli despite the widespread doubts about its viability among many transport planners and professionals. There had long been discussion of a high-speed line north of London, but it was firmly rejected in the mid noughties when Alistair Darling was transport secretary. However, in opposition, the Tories began to put forward the idea and it was picked up by Lord Adonis, who was Labour's transport secretary in the party's final years of government. He created a government company, HS2 Ltd, to draw up a scheme to link London with Birmingham and the North. However, the study started from the wrong place. Instead of assessing the current state of the railway, its bottlenecks and the best way of making improvements, the focus was solely on a high-speed line. Moreover, because it was announced in tandem with the Labour government's commitment for a third runway at Heathrow, the line was routed west-wards out of London to ensure it could connect with the expanded airport rather than, as would have been more logical and shorter, northwards.

On assuming power as part of the coalition in 2010, the Tories, who had put forward a different route, en-dorsed the Labour idea and began to invest serious re-sources into drawing up detailed plans. Because there was support from all three main parties – the Lib Dems were hooked too – there was very little discussion of the fundamentals behind the project. However, its *raison d'être* kept changing. The claims for the line's environmental credentials, such as reducing the need for short-haul flights or reducing fuel consumption, did not survive close scrutiny. HS2 Ltd's own prelimi-nary report suggested a range of greenhouse gas out-comes with a median of approximately no effect. Nor could time savings justify the line's construction. Its supporters, realizing that promoting the line as saving half an hour or so for travellers between London and Birmingham was not winning over sceptics, switched the focus of justification for the line. It was, they now argued, needed in order to increase capacity between London and the major cities of the North and would help to bridge the north–south divide. That, too, has been challenged because research by Professor John Tomaney found that similar schemes elsewhere have tended to favour the larger, already more prosperous, urban centre rather than the smaller cities at the other end of the line.

The politicians, therefore, had to rely on having a strong business case. Only there wasn't one. Despite the numbers sounding good – 'HS2 will bring £15 billion benefits to the economy', according to a study by KPMG – the fundamental business case remained poor. For the line to Birmingham, the benefit–cost ratio remained just below 2, which, by the standards normally applied by the Department for Transport, meant the scheme was moderately good value. While the ratio improves for the whole scheme to around 2.7 (the ratio remains something of a moveable feast and it is giving the system too much credit to accord these numbers a precision that cannot be justified by the methodology), that still remains a poor basis for such a massive amount of expenditure.

Moreover, the very nature of the methodology has trapped the promoters into making suboptimal decisions in an effort to squeeze out a better benefit–cost ratio. The emphasis on time savings means that the line has very few stations and the stations it has are poorly sited, with five (if one includes Crewe) of the nine being on the fringes of the urban areas they are designed to serve, making them far less useful for passengers. The other four, incidentally, are terminus stations, which are far less useful than through stations as they serve fewer destinations and require much longer turnaround times. The need for speed has prevented, for example, the obvious step of buying off the Chiltern protesters with a station to serve them because that would slow the trains down, damaging the business case. It has also led to the line being built to the insanely fast standard of 400 kph, a speed used by no other line in the world and which would require massively increased energy consumption over the 300 kph that is standard on most high-speed lines elsewhere.

Finally, there is an enormous logical contradiction at the heart of the business case. A large proportion of the time savings accrue to travellers who would otherwise have taken conventional trains. They are based on the notion that time spent on trains is regarded by passengers as wasted. In fact, with the widespread use of mobile technology, business travellers can use their time on trains very profitably and those making a leisure trip can also watch a film or read a book, time for which they do not really need to be notionally compensated. Ministers have refused to rework the methodology on this basis, knowing that it would struggle to pass the normal departmental criteria. HS2 is a political project pushed through as a *grand projet* by politicians for reasons that do not stand up to analytic scrutiny. In effect, it is transport policy on a whim.

Chapter 7

It's the politics, stupid

This is not a polemic against the car. Nor against technology. It is, rather, an argument for the development of a genuine transport policy, not the haphazard flailing about that has long characterized the actions of transport ministers. It is not too far-fetched to say that there never has been a transport policy in the UK. John Prescott's White Paper came closest but was killed off by what he called the 'teenyboppers' of Number 10, terrified of the motoring lobby.

Any coherent policy has to start with the appropriate use of motor vehicles, especially in urban areas. We would not start from where we are now if we were given a blank sheet on which to create a transport policy. The notion of allowing a free-for-all on roads – a scarce and finite resource – makes no sense economically, socially or environmentally.

One of the ironies of the availability of new technology in transport, highlighted in chapter 5, is that its most potentially transformational use has largely been ignored. Modern information and communications technology allows for variable pricing, which means that parking or train tickets could be priced differentially according to the time of day or year. For that reason, the low-cost airlines are not always low cost – try booking a summer August Saturday on Ryanair or easyJet to a Mediterranean resort! Yet the most obvious use of this technology would be for road pricing. Roads are a scarce resource, which, as mentioned previously, are free at the point of use: a practice that makes any self-respecting economist tear their hair out. There are exceptions, of course, such as the London and Stockholm congestion charge zones, motorways in countries like Italy and France, various bridges and tunnels, and even the odd turnpike in the US, but they represent a tiny fraction of the world's road network.

However, for the most part, roads suffer from the tragedy of the commons. Rationing is by congestion rather than price. Their usefulness in economic terms is eroded away by congestion and overuse. Free roads ensure that transport provision is suboptimal. This is, though, a political rather than a technological failure. The government in Singapore has managed to impose a comprehensive road pricing system thanks to the fact that, according to *The Economist*, the city state has both 'democratic' and 'authoritarian' aspects. It is, seemingly, the latter that are needed to impose road pricing. In the UK, both Edinburgh and Manchester tried going down the democratic route, asking local voters to decide on charging for road access, only to be comprehensively rebuffed, partly because of fervent media campaigns against the measure. Ken Livingstone managed to impose the charge without seeking a prior mandate, but was re-elected after its imposition, not least because few people ever drove into central London anyway.

Parking, too, is not charged for efficiently, in the precise economic meaning of the term. In most urban areas, there is paid parking, though in an effort to lure people to town centres some local authorities adopt a 'free' parking policy in their multi-storey car parks to match the provision at large out-of-town superstores. There are pressures, too, on public services such as town halls and hospitals to provide 'free' parking. However, even where parking is charged for, the methods tend to be crude, often with a fixed charge irrespective of the time of day or the demand in particular districts where there are popular amenities. While controlled parking zones have been introduced in many residential areas, they are still limited to areas under pressure from outsiders seeking to park to commute or shop. Most people in the UK can still park outside their front door for free, and it is precisely because many see it as a fundamental right that local authorities have often been reluctant to begin charging for what is, again, a scarce resource. The truth is that if parking were paid for at market rates, it would be unaffordable in large swathes of many urban areas.

The solutions lie with the politicians. The question that they never address – and one with which I have teased newly appointed transport ministers in the past – is: do we need more transport or less? The answer, of course, is that we need more of the right sort of transport and less of the wrong sort. That is not an easy concept for politicians to stomach. They are terrified of being seen to limit choice or to prevent people exercising their democratic freedoms. This leads to ridiculously ill-informed policy decisions. Several ministers I have spoken to have been aghast when I suggest that, just possibly, making it more difficult for people to have lager-fuelled stag parties in Riga or Sharm el-Sheikh is hardly an onerous restriction. On the one hand, they recognize the problems – ranging from climate change to congestion – of not charging the real costs for transport, yet on the other they are terrified of doing anything that is perceived as imposing extra costs on travellers.

To formulate a coherent policy requires a better understanding of what transport is for. Ever since the invention of the railways, transport has largely been about mobility rather than access. The distinction is key. Mobility is the means to an end, accessibility is that end. While a few journeys are made for the sake of it, such as on a heritage railway or a cycle ride into the country, most travel is to get somewhere, not for the journey itself – contrary to the picture always given by car ads, showing people travelling on uncluttered roads.

Once the distinction between mobility and accessibility can be understood, a coherent transport policy can be developed. It is not about waiting for the right technological development. The motor car was supposed to bring about many of the freedoms now being suggested by the promoters of driverless cars. The fundamental error of transport policy based on the spread of the automobile is precisely that it was designed to increase mobility rather than accessibility, and it resulted in planning policies that then actually reduced accessibility for many people.

The negative aspects of decades of car-based policy, such as the crowding out of other road users and the encouragement of urban sprawl, which, in turn, entrenched the car's primacy, were all too easily ignored. The car provided fantastic extra mobility for those who could afford to own one, but by destroying alternatives the options available to those who did not were greatly restricted. And, even more ironically, as cars increased in number, their advantages began to be outweighed by their disadvantages.

That is why the emphasis of a future transport policy needs to be on accessibility rather than mobility, a requirement that is all the more important as people increasingly gravitate to live in cities rather than rural areas: for the first time in world history more than half the globe's population are now urban, and that proportion is set to increase in coming decades. It is not an easy distinction to make because, while mobility is quite simple to measure – in terms of, say, passengers per hour or distance to travel – accessibility is a more subtle idea. It is not only about how far people may be from particular facilities such as schools, workplaces, hospitals and so on, but also what is their means of getting there. Websites of both commercial and public organizations often merely state that their facilities are five or ten minutes from, say, a town centre, but that assumes people have access to cars. Those who cannot drive may find it takes far longer to access the facility in question. Therefore, the task for transport planners is to no longer go for simplistic solutions but to base their decisions on very thorough knowledge of their impact. Rather than simple benefit–cost equations based on macroanalysis, a far more complex but robust methodology based more on microdata is required.

The elephant in the room is, of course, climate change. No coherent transport policy can ignore it. Transport contributes around a quarter of the greenhouse gases emitted in the UK and yet is rarely a consideration when developing schemes. While the cost–benefit methodology does place a negative value on emissions, this is generally a small consideration in appraisals and is certainly not a key determinant. Otherwise, many major road schemes (which, as we have seen, are known to generate traffic) and HS2 (which offers no reduction in greenhouse gas emissions) would not come under consideration. Climate change is treated as a minor factor in appraisal rather than, as it should be, a core determining force. Indeed, it should be the starting point for a transport policy.

There also needs to be a coherent approach towards the issue of congestion. The best way to reduce the overuse of roads is to cut demand, through providing alternatives. If the twin drivers of transport policy are climate change and congestion reduction, then the solutions are all too obvious. There have to be supply side measures, such as better public transport and the encouragement of walking and cycling – in Germany, cycle motorways are being built, enabling fast cycling over distances of around twenty to thirty kilometres, very achievable even for the moderately fit if there is no stopping and starting. On the other hand, there must also be measures controlling demand, such as road user charging and road tolling, realistic taxes on aviation to discourage stag parties in Estonia, higher parking charges, a more accurate relationship between carbon emissions and price, and so on.

Cycling

Nowhere is the failure of coherent thinking on transport more apparent than in relation to cycling. For the first two or three decades after World War II, cyclists were seen, like trams and trolleybuses, as a nuisance to the smooth progress of motorcars. Literally thousands of them were mown down. The pre-war statistics were quite astonishing. In the worst year, when 7,343 people were killed on the roads, more than a fifth of these – 1,536 – were cyclists. During the wartime blackout, the high death rate of cyclists was put down by the authorities to their failure to look behind them. With this sort of attitude, it is not surprising that cycling levels reduced year on year, with no effort to keep cyclists on the road. (There were very occasional exceptions, e.g. the excellent cycle routes built on the side of a few new dual carriageways in the 1930s (such as the Great West Road, the A4 out of London), but these soon fell into disuse and efforts to have more such paths were hampered by the domination of the main campaign, the Cycle Touring Club, by fundamentalists who were opposed to separate provision for cyclists, arguing that they ought to have the right to be on all roads.) Cycling after the war was actively discouraged by transport ministry, and while the number of deaths fell, the rate per million miles increased as more and more cars came onto the road.

This was, incidentally, in marked contrast to situation in the Netherlands, where there was, until the early 1970s, a similar decline in cycling use. However, as the number of deaths among children increased, a campaign was started to 'Stop the murder of our children': of the

3,264 deaths in 1973 (a remarkably high number for a country with a quarter of the population of the UK), 450 were of children. This stimulated a campaign to improve facilities for cyclists with safe segregated routes, and a master plan for cycling was produced by the ministry of transport. As a result, cycle use in Amsterdam, which had been declining for years, began increasing gradually from around 1977 to reach the high volumes seen today. This demonstrates that the prevalence of cycling in the Netherlands is not, as is often argued, because it is flat or because it is part of an ingrained culture but, rather, because politicians decided that cycling should be prioritized.

Cycling in Amsterdam.
Source: photo by Steven Lek (see page 115 for full details).

This has never happened in the UK. In Britain, the first tentative measures towards providing for – rather than attempting to ban – cyclists were made in the late 1970s but they were perceived as controversial. Astonishingly, when the Greater London Council, which had installed rudimentary cycle lanes on some major routes, was abolished in 1986, Kensington and Chelsea actually ripped them up, with the council leader, Nicholas Freeman, arguing that cyclists had no place on the roads as they got in the way of motorists.

While that attitude may be extreme, this type of thinking does partly explain the failure of the British government to develop and support a coherent long-term cycling strategy. The contrast with the Netherlands could not be sharper. The nearest we have come to a master plan is a series of central government initiatives that are called 'strategies' but amount to little more than aspirations. The 1996 National Cycling Strategy, launched by Steve Norris, one of the few transport ministers who actually understood the advantages of cycling, promised to double the modal share of cycling journeys by 2002, but it did not set out a road map of how to achieve that. The Labour government replaced that strategy with Cycling England (on whose board I sat) and for a three-year period provided funding of £60 million, which was used to stimulate cycling in a series of demonstration towns and to roll out the Bikeability programme, the replacement for the cycling proficiency test. While this by no means provided sufficient funds for a nationwide programme to boost cycling, it did provide some concrete examples of how it could be done.

In a fit of 'not invented here', Philip Hammond, the first transport secretary in the subsequent coalition government elected in 2010 abolished Cycling England while still claiming to maintain support for cycling. A series of announcements ensued, usually made by David Cameron wearing a cycling helmet, but while there has been support for the occasional project, the government crucially has no budget line solely dedicated to expenditure on cycling

While a few towns with a tradition of cycling, such as Cambridge, York and Chelmsford, have experienced continued growth, the one city to benefit from considerable cycling investment has been London, where a massive increase in cycle use, stimulated from the grass roots largely by young people commuting to the central zone, has almost forced local politicians to respond. On some city centre streets, cyclists became the dominant users in rush hour. A few boroughs responded by installing cycle routes but many of these were inadequate or took users on a circuitous route.

There was, however, a breakthrough in 2012, when the mayor, Boris Johnson, promised to spend £913 million over the next nine years on cycling. Although on examination some of this money was wishful thinking and there was considerable initial underspending on the allocation, it did represent a statement of intent and a genuine step change on previous policies. After his first election victory in 2008, Johnson had embarked on an ill-thought-out programme of cycling superhighways that proved to be expensive and poorly designed, which was highlighted by a series of deaths on the main route in east London. In his second term, however, Johnson is delivering two mostly segregated cycle paths that could – if his successor seeks to continue the programme and has the ability to push it through – be the backbone of a series of routes through central London that will revolutionize cycling in the capital and deliver a massive expansion. Interestingly, Scotland's capital, Edinburgh, has one of the best records on investment in cycling, initially allocating 5% of its budget to cycling back in 2012, with a promise of increasing that by 1% every subsequent year, a policy that crucially has cross-party support. As a result, cycling's modal share in the city has increased at least eightfold since the nadir of the early 1980s when it was just 1%.

Are trams socialist?

There is no doubt which country has the most well-thought through and coherent transport policy. Switzerland has a truly integrated system where buses meet trams that are then timed in with trains. The railways work to a clockwork pattern, so that they depart at the same time every hour, and they have enjoyed consistent investment for generations. Switzerland was the first country in the world to enjoy a fully electrified railway and the high quality of its services combined with the relative cheapness of an annual season ticket mean that it has more journeys per head of population than any other country in the world.

There are two key aspects of the Swiss system that underpin its success: it is based on cooperation rather than competition (the derogatory description would be 'monopoly') and it is a product of a highly decentralized political system where much decision making is made at the local level. Although it is difficult to imagine, Switzerland at the beginning of the twentieth century was a poor country and, while it was not a participant, suffered economically from both world wars as the country's trading routes were disrupted. When the economy recovered after World War II, the priority was to ensure that transport facilities were developed quickly and it was seen as inefficient to create services that competed within or between modes. Unrestrained market forces are seen as wasteful.

Transport services are mostly locally controlled and financed. Taxes are levied locally by the communes (*gemeinde*), who keep some 70%, the cantons (20%) and central government (just 10%) – just imagine the Chancellor of the Exchequer's face if that were suggested in the UK.

Moreover, in the hyperdemocratic way of the Swiss, important decisions on local spending are subject to a referendum. The federal government plays an important coordinating role but the services – buses, trams and trains – are provided by a mix of local authorities, the post office and private companies.

At the urban level, Zurich encapsulates the Swiss approach. It has been through many of the same issues as London but has produced very different answers. In the 1950s the municipal authorities began to suggest that trams were getting in the way of motorists and needed to be put in underground tunnels. The idea was for a 'balanced approach' that would enable motorists to access the city centre easily as the roads would be cleared of the

Zurich: the home of rampant socialism?
Source: photo by Roland Fischer (see page 115 for full details).

trams. The plan to make this radical change was put to a vote in 1962 but, despite the support of local planners and councillors, it was rejected by the public because of the cost. A similar second attempt was made a decade later and failed again. Gradually, an alternative sugges-tion emerged, inspired by the 'small is beautiful' concept developed by E. F. Schumacher. Instead of being held up by cars, trams would be given priority, and the system improved. Eventually this was put to a public vote in 1977 and passed narrowly, changing the whole focus of Zu-rich transport policy that remains to this day, as a plan for urban motorways to be built into the city centre was also rejected around this time. The notion of a balanced approach was abandoned. Instead there was an overt-ly pro-public transport ethos. The crucial aspect is that the whole system works in an integrated, seamless way. All rail lines were provided with regular-interval services and were coordinated in such a way that connections were easy and guaranteed. Trains wait for each other when there are delays. Even small outlying towns and villages are given a guaranteed connection. Any settle-ment with just 300 residents, jobs or educational places must be provided with a basic service, within 400 m (or 750 m if there is a rail station nearby). Services normally run from 6 am to midnight at intervals of sixty, thirty or fifteen minutes depending on whether the area is rural, suburban or urban, respectively. Some busy areas have all-night services. The key is standardization of provision and guaranteed service levels, which guarantees very high levels of usage. Consequently, Zurich has the lowest modal share of car transport of almost any city of comparable size in the world.

Paul Mees, in his book *Transport for Suburbia*, sums up why the approach is so successful:

> Zurich's success ... [is] a triumph for public ownership, and for public strategic and tactical planning. Although the private sector does play a role in the ZVV's [*Zürcher Verkehrsverbund*] system, all the system innovations from tram priority to integrated fares to the pulse-timetable system came from public sector bodies.

He points out that many of these initiatives came from the public, not from the experts. It is the highly democratic Swiss system, which gives so much power to the local level, that 'force[s] city, cantonal and national public transport planners to come up with cheaper, more effective ways of competing with the car'.[20]

To counter the argument that such a centralized system has to be bureaucratic, the number of staff actually employed to oversee the Zurich system is tiny. According to Mees, in 2007 just thirty-five people worked to supervise a system used by 10 million people every week. Contrast this with the vast bureaucracy of Transport for London, which has 400 people on annual salaries above £100,000.

Probably the most significant aspect of Zurich's success is that it demonstrates that low density is not a barrier to the provision of good public transport. Zurich's transport covers large areas where the overall density is as low as thirty-two people per hectare, on a par with suburban areas in American cities. The success of the transport system is, as with cycling in the Netherlands, down to politics and institutional arrangements not to demography or topography.

And Switzerland unequivocally provides the answer to the question in this book's title: are trams socialist? The best tram systems in the world are in Switzerland, a country whose last socialist resident was probably Lenin, before he took that famous train ride, and whose governments are perennially rather right of centre. Trams are a collective form of transport that is economically efficient. Oddly, it is the roads that are run on a socialist basis, as they operate like the queues for fresh bread in Soviet Russia.

This is not a sensible way of allocating resources. Investing in trams or indeed in better bus services such as the now very widely adopted system of Bus Rapid Transit would be a far more efficient use of the limited funds available for transport investment. It would not, though, be socialism.

The Swiss experience, too, suggests that perhaps we can be a bit more optimistic about how a democratic system can deliver a coherent transport policy without the authoritarian approach of Singapore, or indeed of China, which is beginning to recognize the damaging impact of its support for the motorization of its cities and to take measures such as banning private cars on bad smog days.

Instead, one could envisage that the new generation of politicians are the sort of people who were brought up with little or no interest in getting a driving licence at seventeen. Imagine, instead, a generation of politicians who begin to wield power and approach the issue in a much more coherent way, understanding the twin imperatives of reducing the impact of climate change and tackling the issue of ever-growing congestion?

For the moment, though, it is possible to characterize the British approach as almost directly opposed to the Swiss system. One example suffices to sum up the absence of any long-term approach. In 1966 and, again, thirty years later, in 1996, bridges were built over the Severn near Bristol to improve links between England and Wales. On neither occasion was it thought to be a good idea to incorporate train tracks to facilitate better rail travel. Instead, trains still go through the four-mile Severn tunnel, the longest in the UK apart from those on High Speed 1, which has such a huge drainage problem that it has massive pumps operating constantly to avoid flooding. Consequently, trains are limited to sixty miles per hour, adding at least a couple of minutes to every journey between the two countries. Contrast this with the construction of the massive five-mile long Øresund bridge linking Sweden with Denmark that was completed in 2000, combining both rail tracks and a motorway.

The British policy approach relies on the encouragement of competition, privatization and a light touch from government, and it is highly centralized, with very little power at the local level. It is, therefore, the institutional structure, the politics and the prevailing culture that explain why Britain fails in terms of its transport policy. All those can be changed over time, though it will not be easy. As mentioned previously, there are some forces pushing us in the right direction. Young people, for example, are less interested in car ownership and driving. More people are living in urban areas, where public transport and sustainable modes are easier and cheaper to provide. Information technology and advances in ticketing methods offer the opportunity to make accessing public transport more efficient and easier. George Osborne's emphasis on decentralization could be seen as a move in the right direction but, unless it is backed with devolution of financial control, it will do nothing to remedy the fundamental flaws in the British system. Any attempt at transformation needs to start with a recognition of our failings and a willingness to address them, as well as a key cultural change. That is probably the hardest bit.

Transport heaven?

While it may be a bit academic to try to define an ideal transport policy given all of the above – as well as the fact that the Conservative government elected in 2015 is unlikely to adopt any coherent approach to the issue – it is nevertheless worthwhile to try to set out some basic thoughts because the mood can change so quickly (for example, HS2 was for many years considered to be utterly unnecessary but then, suddenly, at the end of the noughties it became the favourite policy of all three major parties). The absence of a clear policy is made worse by the short-termism of government in relation to transport, with decisions on taxation or investment made on the basis of narrow and immediate political concerns rather than any long-term assessment of needs or in the context of any overall vision. As I write this, it is being reported that February 2016 was not only the hottest month on record globally, but that it was way off the scale: a statistical outlier. Climate change may still not be at the heart of government policy in the way that it ought to be, but it could suddenly move to centre stage. It may take the odd cataclysmic disaster or a rapid rise in temperature, but at some point climate change will become – like the war did in 1939–45, say – the key determinant of all aspects of government policy.

In that context, it becomes easier to set out a series of principles that would determine a rational and sustainable transport policy. The approach must start with an assessment of what transport policy is for. It is not, most assuredly, simply about creating more infrastructure so that people can travel further and faster. It is, as mentioned above, about accessibility, ensuring that all citizens can reach the places they need to for work, leisure, education, medical care, friendship, and so on. That means a far more subtle approach to targeting transport investment. It also means taking into account inequality. The right transport policy interventions, targeted at deprived areas or groups of people, can be transformational in unexpected ways. Infrastructure investment, currently focused on big projects like a road tunnel under the Pennines and HS2, would therefore be much better targeted on tram schemes in urban areas, which have tremendous regenerative potential, and on simply ensuring that the humble bus offers a decent service to those without cars.

The second key principle must be that demand management is a key component of policy. The concept of 'predict and provide' should be consigned to the intellectual wilderness where it belongs, and instead there should be a policy of trying to minimize the demand for travel through better provision of facilities, planning and appropriate pricing. This would need to be accompanied by a strategy of encouraging people into the most sustainable forms of transport, which, for the most part, means anything but individualized motor transport (and of course air travel, but this is a very small share of domestic transport movements). The most obvious method, of course, would be a universal road charging mechanism, flexible enough to ensure that peak users of busy roads paid the most while those on deserted routes paid little or nothing. Politically, this has proved impossible to implement, but that is partly because politicians have shied away from initiating any kind of sensible debate on the issue. Given that road user charging could start off as revenue neutral if it replaced fuel tax duty, implementation may not be as difficult as politicians assume, especially as the technology is now readily available.

A key part of demand management is the adoption of what are known as 'soft measures'. These are policies that do not involve any investment in hardware but, rather, are aimed at changing behaviour. Initiatives such as Smart Travel schemes, where individual households are presented with their transport options in interviews, are expensive, but they have been shown to bear fruit, with more people using public transport or walking or cycling when they realize what alternatives are available.

A third key principle would be devolution, though this must come with genuine financial independence. It is no coincidence that those parts of the country that have the best record of transport investment, such as London, Scotland and Manchester, are those with a greater say over infrastructure investment priorities. London is the most compelling example. It already had a fantastic network of transport infrastructure, but thanks to devolution and being given control over its finances (plus the added advantage of being able to bully national politicians by arguing that London is a great growth generator and that transport is vital to that growth), it has, since the mayoralty was created in 2000, created a new network of railways (London Overground), massively improved bus services, imposed a congestion charge to help finance improvements, established a large network of hire bikes, created a series of 'cycle superhighways', obtained a promise to be given control of much of the suburban rail network, and has two massive rail investment schemes due to be completed before the end of the decade (Thameslink and Crossrail). This cannot be replicated easily in any provincial cities, obviously, though Manchester – with its greatly expanded tram network and the soon to be realized assumption of control over its bus network – is showing the way. Crucially, though, devolution must go together with money, as otherwise it will be a poisoned chalice.

There is no silver bullet in any of this but the establishment of a transport policy – or even a debate about one – would be a good start. Certainly, as I have argued, waiting for a technological fix is a mug's game. Technology may be a stimulus for improvements but it is no panacea. Transport planners and, indeed, many politicians are fully aware of the inadequacies of the present situation and know many of the answers. They understand the ways in which a far more rational distribution of transport investment could be made, moving away from *grands projets* and 'predict and provide' and towards smaller but locally significant, even transformational, schemes, but

Realpolitik inevitably intervenes. Measures that impact motorists are seen as too controversial, while the lure of the big project is often simply too strong. One day, however, possibly in the not too distant future, the imperative will be to avoid climate change disaster and, more prosaically, gridlock in our cities, and a coherent transport policy will consequently be adopted. Let us hope that it is not too late by then.

Endnotes

1. Quoted in K. Hamilton and S. Potter. 1985. *Losing Track*, p. 73. Routledge & Kegan Paul.

2. C. Reid. 2015. *Roads Were Not Built for Cars*, p. 134. Front Page Creations.

3. P. Bagwell and P. Lyth. 2002. *Transport in Britain: From Canal Lock to Gridlock, 1750–2000*, p. 90. Hambledon Continuum.

4. M. Hamer. 1987. *Wheels Within Wheels: A Study of the Roads Lobby*, p. 36. Routledge & Kegan Paul.

5. Bagwell and Lyth (2002, p. 94).

6. Quoted in C. Reid (2015, p. 58).

7. House of Commons Debates, 9 May 1977, volume 931,983.

8. C. Buchanan. 1963. *Traffic in Towns: A Study of the Long Term Problems of Traffic in Urban Areas*, p. 47. Penguin Special Edition.

9. Preface to Buchanan (1963, p. 10).

10. See Buchanan (1963, p. 62).

11. British Road Federation. 1963. *Towns and Cities*, p. 12. British Road Federation.

12. See Hamilton and Potter (1985, p. 87).

13. Public Record Office, CAB (Cabinet Office), 134/915.

14. See Hamer (1987, p. 68).

15. Standing Advisory Committee on Trunk Road Assessment. 1994. *Trunk Roads and the Generation of Traffic*, p. iii. Department for Transport.

16. D. Henshaw. 1991. *The Great Railway Conspiracy*, p. 51. Leading Edge.

17. C. Austin and R. Faulkner. 2015. *Disconnected: Broken Links in Britain's Rail Policy*, p. 9. Ian Allan.

18. C. Ledgard. 2010. What happened to the 10-year plan. BBC News Website, 18 January (http://bbc.in/1UexE1i).

19. M. Sivak and B. Schoettle. 2015. Road safety with self driving vehicles: general limitations and road sharing with conventional vehicles, p. 7. Report, University of Michigan Transportation Research Institute.

20. P. Mees. 2010. *Transport for Suburbia*, p. 142. Earthscan.

Photo credits